CONTEMPORARY AMERICAN FICTION

## FLOATING

Marian Thurm, author of the novel *Walking Distance* (now available from Penguin), has published stories in *The New Yorker, The Atlantic, Redbook, Mademoiselle,* and elsewhere. Her work has been chosen for several anthologies, including *Best American Short Stories* and *Editor's Choice.* A graduate of Vassar College with a Master of Arts degree from Brown University, she lives in New York City with her husband and two young children.

# Marian Thurm

# Floating

Penguin Books

PENGUIN BOOKS
Published by the Penguin Group
Viking Penguin Inc., 40 West 23rd Street,
New York, New York 10010, U.S.A.
Penguin Books Ltd, 27 Wrights Lane, London W8 5TZ, England
Penguin Books Australia Ltd, Ringwood,
Victoria, Australia
Penguin Books Canada Ltd, 2801 John Street,
Markham, Ontario, Canada L3R 1B4
Penguin Books (N.Z.) Ltd, 182–190 Wairau Road,
Auckland 10, New Zealand

Penguin Books Ltd, Registered Offices: Harmondsworth,
Middlesex, England

First published in the United States of America by Viking Penguin Inc. 1984
Published in Penguin Books 1988

"Markings" appeared originally in *The Atlantic Monthly;*
"Grace" in *Fiction Network* magazine; "Aftermath" in
*Mississippi Review;* "Floating," "Winter," "Skaters,"
"Secrets," "Still Life," and "Starlight" in *The New Yorker;*
"Light-years" in the *San Jose Mercury News;* and "California" in *Redbook,*
under the title "The Best Thing That Ever Happened."

Grateful acknowledgment is made to Screen Gems-EMI
Music, Inc., for permission to reprint a selection from
"Up on the Roof" by Carole King and G. Goffin.
Copyright © 1962 by Screen Gems-EMI Music, Inc.,
6920 Sunset Boulevard, Hollywood, California 90028.
All rights reserved.

LIBRARY OF CONGRESS CATALOGING IN PUBLICATION DATA
Thurm, Marian.
Floating.
Contents: Floating — Winter — Starlight — [etc.]
I. Title.
[PS3570.H83F5    1988]    813'.54    87-29165
ISBN 0 14 01.1072 0

Printed in the United States of America by
R. R. Donnelley & Sons Company, Harrisonburg, Virginia
Set in Garamond

*For George*
*And also for Frances Kiernan*

# *Contents*

# Floating

*T*he radio claims it is ninety-one degrees, but probably it is hotter. Even the twelve-year-old black-and-white mutt, Oreo, is in the pool, swimming quietly near the diving board. Lynn is lying on her back on an inflatable raft shaped exactly like a giant open hand. The hand is flesh-colored, except for the transparent blue fingernail on the third finger, which you can use to look straight through to the bottom of the pool if you want to. Lynn is wearing maternity jeans that she cut down into shorts at the beginning of the summer, and a red T-shirt, size Extra Large, which says "Coke Adds Life" in white letters that have turned pink from the chlorine. She is twenty-three years old and eight-and-a-half-months' pregnant. She isn't sure she wants a baby, doesn't have a preference about its sex, just wants to give birth to it and work her way back into size-five pants and skirts. After that, who knows? Sharon, her stepdaughter, loves babies; maybe she'll take care of Lynn's baby instead of going back to high school in the fall, and then Lynn will be able to get into an executive-trainee program at Macy's, where she used to work in the perfume department, or go for an MBA at some place like Columbia. Neither possibility seems likely, but Lynn finds herself fantasizing a lot in the pool.

In high school, in Boston, where she grew up, Lynn got straight A's except for math, and ran around with the theater crowd. She was in the chorus of *The Sound of Music,* and of *West Side Story* and *Fiddler on the Roof.* She went to college in Maine, and for a year after graduation she gave piano lessons and cleaned houses. Thinking she had had enough home-grown small-town living to last her forever, she came to New York and got the job at Macy's. It was at Macy's that she met Dan, Sharon's father. He had been trying to decide on a gift for his secretary and had ended up taking Lynn to dinner at a health-food restaurant instead. Over dinner, he told her his wife had died three years before. Dan works for a public-relations firm in the city, but he wants to be a song-writer. Last year, he recorded a demo in a studio, and hired three women for backup. His voice is pleasant, or at least inoffensive, his songs forgettable. Lynn wishes she could tell him to quit while he's ahead, but, on the other hand, she thinks Dan's entitled to his pipe dreams just like everyone else.

For her, marriage and pregnancy have been like something in a dream. She feels no kinship at all with the women who sit alongside her in the waiting room of the obstetrician's office, exchanging stories of backaches and swollen ankles and breasts that are suddenly marked with streaks of violet. And she feels only a distant connection with the baby who is tread-ing water inside her, who stretches his arms and legs a dozen times a day to let her know he's there. She and Dan had been driving back to his house from the city one winter afternoon, fighting heavy rain all the way, when she told him she was pregnant. She had deliberately kept her voice neutral, not wanting to lead him in any particular direction. Mostly be-cause she'd decided she couldn't bear to have an abortion, she had talked herself into going ahead with things, but she wasn't prepared to do the same with Dan. At the least sign of ambiva-lence from him, she would have retreated. But what happened was that he pulled the car off to the side of the road. "Are you serious?" he said, and then he said it again. His mouth stretched toward an unambiguous smile that made Lynn ashamed of her own uncertainty. A few weeks later, she gave up her apartment in the city and moved into Dan's split-level home with a swimming pool in the backyard. They got married shortly afterward, and a month ago she finally quit her job, mostly because she couldn't stand riding the trains and the subways anymore.

As she drifts toward the shallow end of the pool, Lynn's eyes are closed against the sun. Without warning, the baby shifts its weight; a wrist or ankle seems to be struggling to poke its way through. But by the time Lynn's hand reaches her stomach, the little knob of bone has gone deeper underwater and there is nothing to feel.

Sharon is calling to her from the diving board, where she's sunbathing, but somehow Lynn misses most of what she says.

"Are you hungry yet? It's almost three o'clock," Sharon says again.

"Are you?"

"I'll be right there," Sharon says. She dives off the board and surfaces next to Lynn. After she shakes the water from her eyes and adjusts the straps of her bathing suit, she raises Lynn's T-shirt and squints at her belly button, pretending it's a window on the baby. "Hey, you down there," she says, and pulls the shirt back over Lynn's stomach. "I'm making us mushroom omelets. Is that all right?" she asks.

"Thanks," Lynn says. "I thought I was hungry, but I guess I'm not."

Sharon twists her hair into a single wet braid without taking her eyes off Lynn. "How about if I fix it for you anyway, and we'll just see what happens?"

"You're such a little mother," Lynn says, and makes a face, though really she is pleased by all the attention she gets from Sharon. Her stepdaughter is six years younger than Lynn; after lying around the pool together all summer, they have come to think of themselves as the closest of friends. They tell each other things they would never tell Dan: Lynn knows where Sharon's birth-control pills are hidden, and Sharon knows that Lynn sucked her thumb every night in bed until she was fifteen. It is Dan's presence that reminds them that they are not two classmates who just happen to be amiably wasting away a summer together, that they are linked to each other by something more complicated than the mere fact of their having been born in the same decade. Every night when Dan gets home, Sharon disappears into her bedroom, emerging later for dinner, then disappearing again for the rest of the night. Lynn understands that Sharon does not want to be seen being treated like a daughter, nor does she want to see Lynn being treated like a wife.

In the kitchen, butter hisses in a frying pan. Sharon beats the eggs expertly as Lynn pours diet soda into two glasses filled with ice. The odor of eggs cooking in butter is making Lynn sick. The whole house smells of it, and she has to go outside. She lies down on a chaise longue on the patio and calls out to Oreo to keep her company. She whistles for him three times, tosses him his rawhide bone and his squeeze toy shaped like a Popsicle, but he won't come out of the pool. "Go to hell," Lynn says, and then she begins to cry.

Holding the door open, first with her foot, then her shoulder, Sharon backs out onto the patio carrying a large tray with two plates of food, glasses, napkins folded into triangles, silverware, and a bud vase with a miniature pink rose in it. She puts everything down on a wrought-iron table that has an umbrella rising from its center and hands Lynn a glass. "What's wrong?" she says immediately. "You're not feeling well?"

"What could be more pathetic than being rejected by the family dog?" Lynn says, laughing and crying at the same time.

"What are you talking about?"

"Nothing," Lynn says. "I'm crying about nothing."

"I bet it's hormones," Sharon says. "Aren't they all screwy when you're pregnant?"

Lynn shrugs, and drinks from her glass. She wipes the tears from her face with the backs of her hands.

"I thought you were reading up on everything. Didn't you take a whole pile of books from the library?"

"That was Dan. He reads out loud from them every night before he goes to sleep. He thinks it's fascinating."

"I bet it is," Sharon says. "Miraculous, really."

"Miraculous." Lynn mouths the word. She raises her arm over her eyes and hides her face. She is weeping into the crook of her arm, very quietly.

"Is the sun getting to you? We can move into the shade," Sharon says.

Lynn stands up, and when she is able to talk she says, "Have your lunch, and then I'll take you out for a driving lesson. We'll go out to Sunrise Highway and you can practice changing lanes."

"Only if you feel up to it. Otherwise, you can just—"

"Call me when you're ready," Lynn says. "I'm going inside to cool off."

"Me too," Sharon says. She brings the tray into the den and turns on the television set while Lynn settles into a reclining lounger. "Let's be morons and look at cartoons," Sharon says cheerfully. They watch in silence as a dog and a cat and a mouse do their best to wipe each other off the face of the earth. Half an hour later, they go into the garage and get into the front seat of Dan's Cutlass Supreme. (Lynn feels safer in a smaller car and much prefers the Volkswagen Dan leaves at the train station every day.) Sharon is dressed in a dry bathing suit and Lynn in white pants and a green shirt that says "I'm Infanticipating." She hates the shirt but feels obliged to wear it because it was a gift from Sharon.

Behind the wheel, Sharon waits for instructions. "I've never backed out of here before," she explains.

"Just take it slowly and watch out for the hedges when you're in the driveway," Lynn says. A few moments later, when the rear fender is scraping loudly against the privet, she says, "Will you watch what you're doing!"

"Sorry," Sharon says, but she sounds insulted.

It's a delicate business, teaching someone to drive, Lynn thinks. When she was Sharon's age and her father took her around the neighborhood to practice for her road test, it usually ended badly—with both of them in a rage. Her father was always telling Lynn that a car was a weapon and that that was the single most important thing she had to know about driving. When she passed her test on the first try, he hadn't seemed pleased. "Just remember that a car is a weapon that can kill," he said gloomily as he handed her the keys for her first solo trip. "If you're not careful, you can wind up in serious trouble." It took her a long time to fully recover from his teaching methods; for months, she was uneasy behind the wheel, expecting trouble at every corner. This spring, when she wrote her father to say she was pregnant and married, he responded with a check for two thousand dollars. With the check was a note: "Who would believe a girl with such an expensive education could get herself in a mess like this?"

A block from home, Sharon eases the car to a full stop at a blinking red light.

"Very nice," Lynn says. Wherever she looks, there are children playing in the street, roller-skating and tossing Frisbees and riding bicycles. Already she can see blood on the fender. She wishes there were a seat belt that would fit comfortably around her.

Soon they are on the highway, which is cluttered with gas stations and fast-food restaurants and small shopping centers. Sharon is driving well, changing lanes carefully and keeping up with traffic. Lynn switches on the radio and sings along with an old James Taylor song. One spring when she was in college, his voice was everywhere, drifting through open dorm windows out onto the quad, where she had sat typing papers under an oak tree a century old. Where had Dan been then? Probably riding the train back and forth to work, still grieving for the wife he had lost, silently composing his love songs while the rest of the commuters were reading their newspapers.

At their first meeting, Lynn had been very impressed with Dan. He had just got back from a week's vacation in St. Croix, and he looked as handsome as a model in a magazine ad. (She is always surprised at how poorly he photographs; the only expression he can manage is something caught halfway between a smile and a smirk.) She had guessed Dan was in his early thirties, and was stunned when he said he had a sixteen-year-old daughter. He appeared to be very articulate, and everything he said was slightly self-deprecating and ironic—a manner she felt comfortable with immediately. It turned out they were both interested in music and in the theater, and even before they finished their dinner she made up her mind that she would sleep with him. Afterward, in her apartment, they took a long shower together, and made cinnamon toast in the tiny windowless kitchen that was hardly wide enough for the two of them. They spent the hours until dawn going through her Cole Porter songbook, Dan singing while Lynn played the piano her father had shipped down to her from his house in Boston. The next morning, there was a note under her door from the man who lived beneath her. The note said, "One more noisey night, young lady, and I'm calling the cops for sure." Dan corrected the misspelling and circled the word with a red pen. He and Lynn went down to the neighbor's apartment and taped the note to his door, the two of them laughing so hard they could barely stand straight. During his lunch hour that afternoon, Dan showed up at Macy's with a gift for Lynn—a two-record set of Cole Porter singing and playing his own songs. After that, he could do no wrong in Lynn's eyes. (Her first and only other lover, a teaching assistant in the economics department at school, had persisted in buying her little ceramic animals, each one with the same dopey, lovesick look on its face.)

It wasn't long before she was certain that what she had with Dan added up to something close to love, though neither of them ever called it that. She was uncomfortable with the word anyway; it seemed to make too many promises that couldn't possibly be kept.

She was the first of her friends to marry, and when they asked her what it was like, she didn't tell them that even thinking about the subject made her go numb—all she did was smile. The truth is that her friendship with Sharon is more real to her than her marriage and pregnancy. She loves Dan, but living out her life in his house as a wife and a mother and a stepmother is something else entirely.

They are in one of two adjacent left-turn lanes when she hears Sharon say that she thinks she's had enough for the day. The light changes and then suddenly the Cutlass is turning wide and carelessly into the rear end of a gleaming blue Continental. Lynn's arms immediately cradle her middle, though the impact is slight. The blue Continental pulls over into the parking lot of a big sporting-goods store, and Sharon pulls the Cutlass in behind it. Once they are out of the car, they see that no one is hurt, but the front end of the Cutlass is dented and one headlight shattered. The other car has nothing worse than a few dents and some cracked plastic. The driver, a woman, comes toward them, pulling a girl about Sharon's age by the arm.

"Do you see?" the woman says. "This is my daughter—the one who had the three-thousand-dollar nose job last month. If that nose isn't as perfect as it was before this accident, you'll be paying for it the rest of your lives."

"Ma," the girl says, her face bright with embarrassment, "I'm all right, I'm fine."

Sharon clings to Lynn.

"We need the name of your insurance company," Lynn says.

"What do we have here?" the woman says. "The unwed mother and her teenybopper sister?"

"Ma," the girl says again. She turns to Lynn. "It was her new car. She wouldn't even let me or my brother drive it around the block."

Lynn nods. "We're really sorry." She touches the back of Sharon's head.

"I hope your baby's all right," the girl says.

"What about you and your nose?" her mother says darkly.

"I said I was okay. We're all okay. Why do you have to act like such an idiot?"

Swiftly her mother grabs her wrist. "Like it or not, I'm the only mother you've got, kiddo. I'm sorry you think I'm an idiot, but that's the way it is." Turning to Lynn, she says, "It's no picnic, let me tell you."

"I think I ought to give you the name of our insurance company," Lynn says.

The woman says, "Once they hit their teens, you've lost them forever." She closes her eyes. "I was in labor with Bonnie for over thirty-six hours. Back labor, too. The worst kind."

"Could you just shut up, please," Sharon yells.

"Another one," the woman says, and rolls her eyes. "It's a little late to start thinking about protecting your sister, isn't it? Why weren't you thinking about your sister five minutes ago, when you came crashing into us?"

"She's not my sister. She's my stepmother," Sharon says.

The woman's mouth opens wide. "Jesus Christ."

A police car with its siren on is headed their way. In a few moments, two cops pull into the parking lot. "Anyone need an ambulance?" one of them asks. "You?" He points a finger at Lynn's stomach.

"I'm fine," she says.

"We're all just fine," Bonnie says.

They are back in the pool when Dan gets home. It is after seven, and the air is as hot as it was all day, the water in the pool as warm as bathwater. Lynn is on the raft, her hands clasped over her stomach. Sharon is doing a handstand near the shallow end, her legs perfectly straight and still above the water. Dan kneels at the edge of the pool and pulls the raft toward him. He kisses Lynn's stomach, then her mouth.

"Hard day at the office?" he says, and laughs.

Sharon is swimming underwater now, close to the floor of the pool. "We had an accident—nothing too serious," Lynn says. "Broken headlight, dented fender—that kind of accident."

"Were you thrown forward? What about the baby?"

"Nothing happened. And anyway, babies in utero are well protected from the outside world. I could be shot in the stomach right now and the baby would be fine."

Dan flinches. "Maybe you ought to go see the doctor anyway."

Lynn shakes her head. She is watching Sharon at the bottom of the pool. "Poor kid," she says. "She's been a real space cadet since it happened. Why don't you take her out to dinner or something?"

"We'll all go," Dan says. "All three of us."

"I'm not very hungry. And the two of you should spend some time together alone," Lynn says.

"What about tomorrow? I'll make us some omelets tonight."

"When are you going to take a look at the Cutlass?"

"Later," Dan says. "After the sun goes down and it's too dark to see anything."


It is sweltering the following afternoon, when Lynn and Sharon drive the Cutlass over to the service station. The manager promises it won't take more than an hour to replace the headlight, and he offers to let them wait in his office—the only part of the station that's air-conditioned. For nearly two hours, they sit on molded plastic chairs reading year-old copies of *Reader's Digest.* Twice, Sharon goes out front to the soda machine and returns with paper cups of lukewarm Tab and a progress report on the car. "They'll be getting to it shortly, whatever that might mean," she tells Lynn. To pass the time, Sharon reads aloud from "Laughter, the Best Medicine" and "Life in These United States" and searches for the dumbest things she can find. After a while, Lynn settles back in her chair, her mouth open slightly. When the car is finally ready, Sharon has to wake her. They drive straight home.

That night, Sharon and Dan eat at the Hello Deli. Lynn is too tired to go out; for dinner she has a large bowl of mocha-chip ice cream, which she eats very slowly with a demitasse spoon. Wearing headphones, she listens to most of her Cole Porter album, then goes to sleep at around nine, without Dan, who still hasn't got back from dinner. At two, she is awakened by a cramp in her abdomen; then suddenly the mattress underneath her is flooded with warm water. She turns on the reading lamp over the bed and Dan begins to stir.

"What?" he says.

"My water broke," she says, and slides toward the edge of the bed.

"Don't move!" Dan yells. He races from the room and returns carrying newspapers, which he opens and spreads all around the bedroom floor and out in the hallway. "You can get out of bed now if you want to," he says, and as she stands water spills onto the paper. "Just didn't want you to wreck the carpet."

Lynn stares at Dan. "Call the doctor," she says.

She goes into the shower and washes her hair, forgetting that she washed it after she got back from the service station, not many hours ago. Her mind is a perfect blank, but her legs are trembling on the tiled floor of the stall shower. She dries her hair in the bedroom with a dryer that looks just like a Colt .45, watching Dan in the mirror as he gathers her bathrobe and toothbrush and some nightgowns together in a canvas bag for her. In his hand he holds a checklist from the hospital. "Cards," he says. "We need a deck of cards."

"We don't *play* cards," Lynn says. "What are you talking about?"

"If it says to bring cards, we should." Dan pauses. "Shouldn't we?"

"Why don't you go wake Sharon?"

"We can leave her a note," Dan says.

"I want her to come with us."

"She's just a kid in high school. What do you want from her?"

Without answering, Lynn gets dressed and goes downstairs to Sharon's room. The first contraction comes as Lynn calls Sharon's name. In the dark, Sharon sits up against the head-board. "I'm so afraid," Lynn whispers as Sharon reaches for her.

Riding in silence on empty parkways to the hospital, Lynn can't stop thinking about something a friend of hers who was in medical school told her—a story about a baby who was born with one eye in the center of its forehead, a full set of teeth, and shoulder-length hair; when it was wheeled down to be X-rayed, the technician fainted.

"Perfect parallel park," she hears Dan say as he backs the car neatly into a space on York Avenue. "I hope you were paying attention, Sharon."

"I'm not getting out of this car," Lynn says. "I'm in the mood to ride around a little."

"In the mood?" Dan says. "You're supposed to be in the mood to have a baby."

"Not right now," Lynn says. "In a little while, maybe."

Dan turns to Sharon, in the backseat. "Will you talk to your friend, please?" he says.

"When she's ready, she'll go," Sharon says.

"I'm trying very hard to understand what's going on here, but it's just not working out," Dan says.

Lynn says, "You know, I've never actually seen Gracie Mansion. Why don't we take a ride over there?"

Dan sighs. "One quick look, and that's all."

.     .     .

There's a color TV in the labor room, and together Lynn and Dan watch the best of late-night programming—a Troy Donahue surfing movie that was filmed on location in Hawaii and seems to go on forever. Toward daylight, just as Fred Flintstone is being berated by his wife for never taking her anywhere interesting, Lynn is rushed to the delivery room across the hall, where she propels their child into the world with a final push that distorts her face unrecognizably. Moments later, she asks for Sharon, who is waiting downstairs on a wooden bench in the lobby.

"Go down and get her," Lynn tells Dan.

"Why would they let her into the delivery room?" Dan says. "That's crazy."

"I want her here," Lynn says. "Get her." She raises her head and watches Dan and the obstetrician whispering at her feet.

Afterward, with Sharon standing shyly against the door, the doctor congratulates them all, and says to Dan, "You may now kiss the bride." Then Dan is leaning over her, a green paper mask still covering his mouth, and in a voice she's never heard before, a voice belonging to someone else, Lynn says to her husband, "Don't."

# Winter

*E*veryone said Harte would hardly remember a thing, that it would all be a blur in her mind and that she would need an album full of pictures to show her the way it had been. But six months after the wedding the details are still fixed firmly in her memory: the dry rustle of her gown against the carpet as her father guides her down the aisle, past her mother's friend who leans out from her seat and hisses, "Smile, this is a wedding, not a funeral," the staccato clicking of the photographer's equipment all through the ceremony, the sweet look of contentment on Brian's face that makes her want to drop kisses beneath his cheekbones as they dance their first dance together as husband and wife.

It had been a hot, damp night and the first thing she did when she got into the car was take off her pantie hose, slinking down almost to the floor as Brian kept watch from behind the steering wheel. Then they had driven to a hotel in Manhattan. In a small, square green-and-gray room, which would have been a disappointment to anyone except a salesman in town on a business trip, they stayed up past dawn counting the checks that had been tucked inside the pockets of Brian's tuxedo—checks for fifty, seventy-five, and, less frequently, one hundred dollars.

By now the checks have all been spent on tuition for Brian's third year in medical school, and Brian and Harte are living in a university town in Florida, in a garden apartment ten minutes from the hospital where Brian does his clinical training. Harte hates the smallness of the town, and the dull, hot days that are easily wasted away. After a half year of marriage she does not know what there is to say for her life. Every week her mother calls her long-distance from New York and asks questions, and Harte feels like weeping. She does not know how to explain that nothing is happening to her, that her days are as motionless as the water in the neighboring swamp.

Three years ago, when Harte first met Brian, he seemed the only person she knew who was confident about his future. He was in his last year at Harvard, with four applications filed for medical school, and every weekend he waited for her at South Station with a rose wrapped in waxy green paper. One night, late in April, as she sat curled drowsily in his darkened room, he played "Suzanne" for her on his guitar, sounding just like Leonard Cohen, and convincing her that it was all somehow connected with love.

Immediately after his graduation, Brian drove home with his parents, who had retired and moved from Ohio to a suburb of Miami. Because he was now an official resident of Florida, Brian's medical-school tuition would be as low there as it could possibly be anywhere. And that, he explained to Harte, was the one good reason for putting a thousand miles between them. He called her every Sunday night that summer and wrote her two or three times a week, though as soon as school began the letters became postcards and he occasionally forgot to mention how much he missed her. Harte kept his letters and postcards in a shoe box, but only the romantic ones—the rest she stuffed into the compactor under the sink.

She started school in the fall, enrolling in a graduate program in English at Columbia, which was what she had planned to do before she met Brian. Sometimes she wondered why he hadn't asked her to alter her plans and come down South for graduate school. He never even seemed close to suggesting it, and if the subject of her going to Columbia came up, he always said that it was an excellent school and that he was glad she had the opportunity to go there. Whenever she heard him say these things, it seemed to her that the balance of love was tipped in his favor, and she began to feel uneasy. But each time she went through the letters in the shoe box the evidence showed that she had no cause to worry.

Thanksgiving vacation of her second year at Columbia, Brian came to visit Harte's family, and he finally admitted that he was tired of carrying on a long-distance romance, that marriage seemed like a good idea to him. They both agreed that once Harte got her master's she would try to find a teaching job in one of the junior colleges near the town where Brian lived. But even as they made plans, Harte did not tell Brian how often she had imagined herself marking her students' papers with a red felt-tipped pen as he lay beside her on their double bed, reading the *New England Journal of Medicine,* his hand resting gently at her neck.

Harte's mother and father did not want her to marry Brian. They said it was because he was self-absorbed and did not pay as much attention to her as he should, but Harte (who knew these accusations had very little truth to them) was sure it was only because they did not like the way she and Brian looked together. Harte is tall and sturdy-looking, with big, wide hands and feet that are much larger than Brian's. When she and Brian stand side by side, it is clear how tall she really is, how broad across the shoulders. Her father even tried to convince her that small men were a breed of their own, saddled with inferiority complexes that they covered up in predictable ways. After that, he said nothing further to dissuade her. The wedding plans were made and carried out, and Brian's new Fiat got them all the way to Florida without overheating once.

In Florida, they settled in the apartment Brian had rented for them, and Harte waited to hear about the teaching jobs she had applied for and tried to get used to the burning summer heat. One afternoon during their first week in the apartment, she nearly blacked out while crossing a parking lot.

On weekends the two of them walked the malls of the handful of small shopping centers nearby, looking at all the things they couldn't afford. Together they went through the racks in the Better Sportswear department of Maas Brothers, the one decent department store in town, and assembled expensive outfits for Harte—pale silk blouses and corduroy skirts and matching jackets with leather buttons. Each time she came out of the dressing room, Brian stood alongside her in front of the mirror in the middle of the floor and adjusted the collar of her shirt or smoothed the shoulders of her jacket and finally grinned at her in the mirror and told her she looked terrific. After she changed back into her dungarees and T-shirt and returned the clothing to the racks, she and Brian would walk over to Baskin-Robbins for frozen chocolate-covered bananas, which came on an ice-cream stick and cost less than a dollar. Now and then, they went to the movies, though the only films playing starred Clint Eastwood or Charles Bronson, or had titles like *The Stewardesses*. "This isn't New York," said Brian when Harte asked where all the good movies were. Later, he said she was suffering from ordinary homesickness and culture shock. He was positive she would feel much more settled and at home as soon as she had a job.

When it was clear that the schools hadn't any openings, Harte began reading the tiny column of want ads in the local paper and convinced herself that working in Burger King or Pizza Hut or as a clerk in a discount drugstore would be better than not working at all. She dressed up in a skirt and tried to look eager as she filled out one application after another for jobs that she could not imagine anyone's ever wanting. At the end of her first week of interviews, the man who took her application at Uncle Jerry's Family Restaurant told her that what he was really looking for was someone who would fit in well with the rest of his employees, who were mostly kids from the high school in town. "We're like a family here," he said, "and I just can't picture you as one of our relatives."

Then, one afternoon in October, Brian called from the hospital with the news that he had found Harte a job as a shelver in the medical library. That night they decided to celebrate and baked a quiche for dinner—their first joint project in the kitchen. They kept laughing and bumping into each other along the narrow length of linoleum, and Harte spilled a frying pan full of sautéed onions into the sink, but the quiche came out perfectly. When they sat down to eat, Brian lit a candle shaped like an ice-cream sundae and turned the lights off for the rest of the evening.

Harte's "poor attitude and general lack of enthusiasm" got her fired from the job six weeks later. After that she couldn't even go to the public library in town and take out books for herself without being reminded of her failure.


It is a sultry January day and Harte is on her way to the supermarket. She drives with the windows rolled all the way down in the dark-blue Fiat that has already turned purplish in the Florida sun. Her hair blows across her mouth in the hot wind. She tries to remember the sound of a shovel scraping snow from the sidewalk outside her parents' house and her father in a red-and-white-striped ski hat, knocking off the row of icicles that hangs every winter under the roof over the porch. In the car perspiration dampens the creases of her arms and her hands stick to the hot plastic of the steering wheel.

She quickly fills her cart at Pantry Pride with cans of SpaghettiOs, boxes of frozen pizza, a carton of Good Humor Whammy sticks, a two-liter bottle of Pepsi, and several kinds of Pepperidge Farm cookies for her friend Sam, the only friend she has made since moving to Florida. Sam, who lives in the apartment above theirs, likes to visit when Brian is at the hospital. Brian does not approve of Sam. He regards him as a bad influence on Harte.

Harte joins the express line, ten items or less. A man directly ahead of her and a woman directly ahead of him are having an argument. The man accuses the woman of pushing her shopping cart in front of his.

"You weren't here," the woman begins reasonably. "You left your wagon. Why should I have stood here like an idiot, wasting my valuable time?"

"What a hustler!" says the man. "You're a real asshole, you know that?"

Reaching into her wagon, the woman grabs a bunch of broccoli and brings it down over the man's head. "See what you get for opening up a mouth like that?" she hollers.

The man stretches his thumb and index finger across his forehead like a visor. "Using a vegetable as a weapon is a felony in the state of Florida," he says. He tells the woman that his brother-in-law is a lawyer. "You're in big trouble," he says. Harte is about to laugh, when he turns on her. "What are *you* looking at?" he says. "Haven't you ever seen anyone assaulted in a supermarket before?"

The girl who works at the checkout counter shakes her head slowly and goes off to get the manager, and Harte abandons her wagon, slipping past the man and his assailant, hugging her arms to her chest, unexpectedly packageless. She drives more than halfway home; then, realizing that it is their six-month anniversary and she has forgotten to buy Brian a card, she heads back to the shopping center.

All the cards in the stationery store are extravagantly sentimental, with photographs of young lovers posed next to the ocean, or close-ups of roses in bloom and rhymed couplets about a love that is deep and true. Finally she chooses one that says "For My Grandson on His Confirmation Day."

In the apartment Harte finds Brian waiting for her. He leans against the kitchen counter, one small bare foot on top of the other, a stethoscope drooping from the pocket of his white coat like the dark stem of a wilted flower. He kisses Harte's shoulder and the back of her neck. "Come and lie down with me on the couch," he says. "I've got to relax for a while."

Harte looks at her watch. "Just in time for a 'Leave It to Beaver' rerun," she says, and she turns on the television before sitting down. Brian rests his head on her stomach and sticks his legs over the arm of the couch.

Beaver is having dinner with his family. His mother orders him to eat the brussels sprouts on his plate, but instead he tucks them into the pocket of his shirt as soon as she turns away. The laugh track goes wild. Brian makes a face at Harte and closes his eyes.

"Why don't you go to sleep?" says Harte. She helps him take off his white coat, pulling his arms from his sleeves like a mother tending her drowsy child. Brian settles down into the couch, his shirt riding up his back, exposing a sweet pale square of skin. The skin is miraculously soft; Harte draws circles around it with her finger as Brian falls asleep.

"I'm so hungry," he says later when he wakes up. "Did you get to the supermarket today?"

"I went to Pantry Pride," says Harte, "but I had to leave without buying anything."

"What's with you?" says Brian. "How could you come home from the supermarket without any food?"

"I'm sorry," says Harte. "Do you want me to tell you what happened?"

"Never mind. I don't think I want to hear about it—we had a cardiac arrest on the ward today. The resident had me go out and break the news to the patient's wife. The first thing she said was 'Oh God, who's going to do my income-tax returns this year? I'll never be able to do them myself.' " Brian rubs his eyes. "I'm not sure I can deal with all the people out there, Harte," he says.

"Sure you can. You can deal with everything." Harte takes the confirmation card out of her knapsack and gives it to Brian. "Happy six months," she says.

Brian reads the card, his face solemn. "Everything is a joke with you," he says quietly. "Can't you take anything seriously? Did your friend Sam tell you to buy this card?"

"What are you talking about?"

Brian studies her for a moment, then runs his fingers along the underside of her arm. "Look," he says, "I think we should do something to celebrate our anniversary. We could drive out to Fat Boy's and have drinks and steak. I have to be back at the hospital by eight, but at least we can celebrate for a couple of hours."

"I don't feel like going anywhere or doing anything. I did a little while ago, but I don't anymore."

"It's the heat," says Brian. "You miss the change of seasons down here. I bet you feel like you've been cheated out of a fall and a winter this year."

"Don't talk down to me," says Harte. "Sam says that was the first thing he noticed about you. He could tell you were planning to specialize in psychiatry just by the expert way you talked down to me."

"I apologize," says Brian. "And we won't talk about Sam anymore."

Harte prepares a tuna-melt sandwich for Brian's dinner and places a delicate pink birthday candle through the layer of American cheese.

"That's a very nice-looking sandwich," says Brian, and blows out the flame after a moment of hesitation. Then he snaps the candle sharply into two pieces and throws them into the sink.

"What did you wish for?" says Harte, looking at the sandwich, which suddenly seems meager on the big yellow plate.

"Nothing too extravagant," says Brian.


In the apartment complex where Harte and Brian live there are tennis courts and a laundromat that are open twenty-four hours a day, but there aren't any married women Harte's age who don't have at least one child. Without Sam, Harte doesn't know what would become of her. Sam lives upstairs with Dizzy, his lover. Dizzy sells expensive running shoes in a shop on the main street, which divides the town in half; actually he is the manager of the store and works long hours six days a week, returning home to Sam too tired to do anything except sit with a pair of headphones on, listening to a tape of the music from *Saturday Night Fever*. The two of them own a borzoi, which Sam walks in the field of tall, bleached grass behind their apartment. Harte met Sam for the first time one afternoon when she was out in the field with her butterfly net, watching the borzoi run in long strides through the grass like a lean and fragile horse, while Sam stood smoking a cigarette, his head tipped skyward. They watched the borzoi together and Sam told her about himself: that he was a medical-school dropout, that after one four-hour session of gross anatomy he knew he had made a terrible mistake. Harte laughed and said she knew *she* had made a terrible mistake when she realized she was living in a town whose finest restaurant was called Fat Boy's Bar and Grill.

Tonight, after Brian leaves for the hospital, Harte climbs upstairs to Sam's apartment. He calls out to her from the bedroom and says, "I'm back here cleaning. I'll be out in a couple of minutes."

There is a record playing on the stereo: Gertrude Lawrence whistling a happy tune on her way to Siam. The record is from 1951 and is full of scratches. Sam stole it from his mother's collection when he left home. He also stole the original Broadway-cast recordings of *Pal Joey, South Pacific,* and *Carousel.* His mother writes him letters twice a month. On the bottom of every letter she writes, "P.S. What about my records? P.P.S. Pardon me for being a nag." Sam has told Harte that his mother might get her records back if she wised up and stopped begging him to get psychiatric help for his "condition," as she calls it.

Harte gets herself a can of Pepsi from Sam's refrigerator. The soda foams in the glass, sprays her nose and mouth as she takes the first sip. She wonders if Brian is right and her teeth will actually soften and fall out one by one because of all the soda she drinks. Brian has already warned her that if they ever

have children, he'll make sure their house stays free of car-
bonated beverages. "So if you want a fix, you'll have to leave
the house to get it," he said, looking so earnest that Harte
leaned forward and turned up the corners of his mouth with
her fingers.

Sam drops down on the carpet in the living room. He is
large-boned and slightly overweight and is wearing a T-shirt
with a subway map of New York City on it. In his lap he holds
a dispenser of Windex, a sponge, a rag, and a plastic bottle of
ammonia.

"If you had one word to describe the look in Brian's eyes,
what would it be?" asks Harte.

"Determined," says Sam immediately.

"Determined to finish medical school, anyway."

"He's lucky he's got the stomach for it."

"Do you know what the third-year students are doing now?
Tracheotomies on dogs and cats."

"That's enough," says Sam. He goes back to his cleaning.
He cleans in places Harte has never even considered: across
the glass face of the clock on the wall, on the molding that runs
below the windowsills, behind the filter in the air conditioner.
He is a skillful and energetic housekeeper, moving from one
task to another only after he's sure he's done all he can. Love
dominates his life; it is love that propels him to keep the
apartment in the perfect order that Dizzy needs to come home
to every night.

Sam knows that running shoes figure most prominently in
Dizzy's life, that Dizzy will always be a businessman with not
much time for love.

Harte wishes that Sam would give up on Dizzy. Once she
dreamed that she and Sam ran away to New York City together and got an apartment down in the Village. Brian
showed up right away with a court order that gave him the
power to take Harte back to Florida. The worst of it was that
Sam, who stood at the doorway grooming his mustache with
a tiny comb, kept repeating "It's all for the best" as Brian tied

her up with string and placed her on the backseat of the Fiat.

As the second side of *The King and I* comes to an end, Yul Brynner gets a dancing lesson from Gertrude Lawrence. Harte, sitting with her ankles crossed in front of her, knocks her feet together in time with the music.

"*The King and I* is my favorite show," says Sam. "Even the happiest songs in it have something mournful about them."

The record is over; Sam flips it back to the first side and starts it again. Later he puts on *Pal Joey* and finishes off two white-wine spritzers. When his second glass is empty, he tells Harte that Dizzy will be home any minute. Harte says that she has to get back to her apartment anyway, pretending that Brian will be calling to make sure she's not feeling lonely.

Brian is on at the hospital every third night in February, and when he's not he likes to be in bed by ten with Harte lying next to him. He says that he can't fall asleep without her, that he panics if she's not within easy reach.

One night, as Brian pulls back the sheets and gets into bed, Harte says, "Before I married you, I never heard of grown people going to sleep at ten o'clock."

"I'm exhausted," says Brian. "Today was awful."

"What happened?"

"I had to tell a patient he had lung cancer. He was a nice middle-aged man, very quiet, very polite; he just kept nodding his head to everything I was saying."

Harte switches off the light and stretches out on her back along the edge of the bed. "Why do you have to tell me stories like that?" she says.

"The man was so polite. He thanked me for talking with him. He shook my hand."

"Don't you know when to stop?" says Harte. "I can't listen to this."

Brian turns toward her. He covers her face with small, soundless kisses. Then, in a moment, it seems, he is asleep.

Harte closes her eyes tightly and pushes them with her fingers, two fingers on each eye. It is an old game: first black becomes red, then there are perfect rows of geometric shapes, silver ones with violet centers. Upstairs, in Sam's apartment, the floor creaks. Something is thrown against the wall. Harte sits up in bed, strains to hear what it is the voices are saying. She thinks she hears her name; a door slams and there is nothing more to listen to, except the sound of Brian breathing evenly beside her, his arm bent across his forehead, his fingers clenched into a fist so small it might belong to a child.

It is early spring, and Harte and Sam have secretly taken up tennis. Several nights a week, while Brian is at the hospital and Dizzy lies on the couch with his headphones on, they spray themselves with insect repellent and head out for the courts. Harte and Sam play very badly. They wait until after midnight to start their games so that no one will see them. Even so, Sam dresses in proper whites and plays with an expensive racquet and a sweatband around his hair.

Their nights on the courts are always the same: the air as warm and damp as the night Harte was married, and the two of them clowning around and calling each other "spastic" and "clod" as they play. One night, though, they are surprised to see two people, a boy with a waist-length ponytail and his girlfriend, whom Harte recognizes from the laundromat, playing on the next court. They have a nice rally going between them as Harte and Sam approach.

"I'm not going to play with them here," says Harte. "We can come back later, if you want."

"I don't mind making a fool of myself. Why can't we just go ahead and play?"

"Wait," says Harte. In a little while, the boy with the ponytail and his girlfriend end their game and come together at the net. The boy bends over his side of the net to embrace the girl. When they break apart, she raises her arm and points overhead to an unimpressive sky, empty of stars.

"What are they looking at?" says Sam. "There's nothing to see up there."

"They're in love. People in love watch for signs."

Sam takes three tennis balls out of a can and tries to juggle them. He drops them all and they roll away in three different directions. He goes after them and when he returns to Harte the couple is walking off the court, each with an arm over the other's back.

"They're so happy," says Harte. "I see them doing their laundry together all the time, and he folds her shirts and nightgowns for her in a way that lets you know there's really something between them."

Sam serves first. He keeps hitting the ball into the net. In the swamp nearby there are frogs jeering at him. A tiny band of them leaps brazenly onto the court. Sam swings at them with his racquet. "Time out for a cigarette," he says.

Harte listens for the sharp metallic click of his lighter. She can smell the smoke that hangs in the air in front of him. "What's the matter?" she says, and walks up to the net.

"I'm so depressed," says Sam.

"Your serve will get better if you keep at it."

"It's my hair," says Sam. He leans over the net. "Feel the top of my head. Can you see how thin it's getting?"

His hair is soft and fine beneath her fingers. She smooths it in place with her knuckles, moving her hand slowly across his head, thinking of the couple embracing over the net, of the romance of their posture.

"What do you think?" says Sam.

"Your hair is nice to touch."

Sam snaps his cigarette onto the court.

"All right," says Harte. "From now on we're going to try and play a real game. No more fooling around. You're going to run up to the ball when I hit it. You're not going to stand there and wait for it to fall at your feet."

"I'm a slow-moving guy," says Sam. "I've never been fast on my feet."

"Get ready to run," says Harte. She serves the ball as powerfully as she can. Sam rushes toward it, a luminous streak of white across the court.

Later, they collapse in their wet clothes in Harte's apartment, savoring their shared exhaustion, drinking Pepsi straight from the bottle, passing it back and forth between them like a pipe full of hash.

Sam turns on the radio. He switches from one station to another until he finds an old Beatles song, melancholy and slow. "Dance with me," he says, and pulls Harte up from the floor. His hand rests at the small of her back. "You're tense," he says with surprise. "Just go with the music."

Harte leans her head on the hard shelf of his shoulder and feels her bones go loose. "See how easy it is," she hears Sam say, and then she closes her eyes. She is dancing at her wedding, without her shoes on, hoping that she and Brian are nearly the same height. Her feet are slipping on the waxed parquet floor. "Easy now," says Brian, and he presses her to his chest, trying to steady her. But she loses her balance anyway, and slips through the circle of his arms around her and out of his reach.

# *Starlight*

*Elaine and her mother had* spent the day shopping, going from one department store to the next—from Lord & Taylor to Saks to Jordan Marsh to Burdines. It was Elaine's third day in Florida, and they had been looking for gifts for her two boys: Jesse, who was nine, and Matthew, who was eleven. Elaine hadn't seen either of them in months, and she hoped the shirts and sweaters she had bought were the right sizes. The last time she saw them was in early December, when she left their house in New Jersey with three large suitcases crammed with her winter clothes. At first she had felt an overwhelming grief when the boys told her they preferred to live with their father; the humiliation had come later, along with a sudden cold anger. She got over her anger soon enough—how could you be angry at children who were too young to know they had hurt you? The grief stayed with her much longer, but she was finally over that, too. It was the humiliation that lingered. As her mother and father had said more than once since Elaine's arrival, "Who ever heard of young children like that just coming right out and picking their father over their mother, no two ways about it?"

Even Peter, Elaine's husband, had been amazed at the boys'

decision. He hadn't been all that pleased about it, either. Keeping Jesse and Matthew meant keeping the house and finding someone to take care of things until he got home from work. It wasn't anything like what he had envisioned for himself. He didn't go into details, but Elaine knew that whatever it was he wanted was going to be harder to get now that there were two children to be looked after. When he first told her why he wanted out, she stared at him in disbelief. She was boring, he said. Nothing she did or said or wanted was interesting anymore. They were on their way back from the city, where they had had dinner with a friend of Peter's from college—a criminal lawyer who specialized in defending celebrities who'd been arrested on drug charges. He had asked them to a big party he was giving, where there was sure to be plenty of really good dope, and Elaine wanted to know why Peter had said they'd love to come, why he'd said it sounded like a great way to spend an evening. We're not college kids anymore, she yelled at him in the car as they crossed the George Washington Bridge. You really are a drag, he said quietly, and he didn't let up until they pulled into the driveway of their house. They sat in the car for what seemed to be hours, Elaine shivering as they talked. What did he want her to do, she asked him. Take up skydiving? Get a job as a trapeze artist? Put a ring through her nose? That's when he told her he wanted out and gave his reasons. Her own reasons, at least, made sense; it was impossible to love someone who criticized her at every opportunity, who belittled her in front of her children, her friends, strangers, the whole world. After thirteen years, she had had enough. Even so, Peter had the last word. Whenever Elaine heard a book or a movie or a TV program described as boring, her skin prickled with goose bumps, as if she were in danger.

"You had a phone call," her father said. He had just unlocked the apartment's four locks to let Elaine and her mother inside.

"Who was it?" her mother said.

"Sweetie, did I say I was talking to you?" her father said.

"Who was it, Daddy?" Elaine said.

"It was Peter. He said the airport in Newark was snowed in, and the kids wouldn't be down until tomorrow. Or maybe the day after. It all depends on the weather."

"Was he civil to you, at least?" Elaine's mother said. She and Elaine put their shopping bags down in the foyer. The apartment was the perfect size for two people, with an L-shaped living room and a kitchen that could only take a small round table. Elaine had been sleeping in the second bedroom her parents used as a den, but once the boys arrived she'd have to camp out in the living room. The three of them went out onto the screened-in terrace. The terrace overlooked the Intracoastal Waterway; just as they sat down, a motorboat went by, buzzing so loudly neither of them caught her father's answer. "Well, was he or wasn't he?" her mother said.

"Bastards," her father said. "I wish those creeps would stay out of my backyard."

"What else did he say?" Elaine asked her father.

"Peter? He was very polite. He asked how all of us were. He said the boys were very disappointed about the trip's being postponed. They can't wait to see all of us. Especially you, Lainie Bug, needless to say."

"Needless to say." Elaine knew her father was lying—his voice sounded unnaturally hearty, as if he were speaking to someone too old or too young to be told anything close to the truth.

"Well," her mother said, "disappointed though we all may be, you can't do anything about the weather, and that's that."

"Thank you, Mother, for your wit and wisdom in these trying times," Elaine's father said.

"Please don't talk to her like that," Elaine said.

"Your mother knows I like to kid around. That's the way I am."

"I don't mind. Or most of the time I don't. After forty years—"

"Well, you should mind," Elaine said. She stood up and looked out over the water at the condominiums that seemed to take up every last square foot of land. Just across the way, a hundred yards in the distance, she could see men and women lounging around a long rectangular swimming pool, and a diver poised on the board, ready to take off. She watched as he flew into the water and disappeared. It was a mistake to have come to Florida, she realized. But the boys had never been here before, and she had wanted to meet them on neutral ground, to vacation with them far enough from home so that she wouldn't have to worry about their calling for their father to come and get them in the middle of the night. And she had wanted to be among allies, people she could count on for comfort if things went disastrously with her children. What she hadn't counted on was her parents' making her feel worse than she'd felt all winter long. Her father was especially hard to take. Since his retirement, he'd mellowed, but she never knew what to expect. It was easy enough to be fond of him from a distance; living with him in such close quarters these past few days, she'd begun to wonder if she'd last the week or end up running out to find herself a motel.

The telephone rang.

Her mother said, "Arthur?"

"Don't look at me," her father said. "I'm just sitting here enjoying the view from my terrace."

"If it's for you, I may just hang up."

"Suit yourself."

Her mother picked up a phone that was on the terrace floor, next to a seven-foot-tall cactus. "Brenda," she said after a moment. "It's not bad news, is it?" She carried the phone past the sliding glass door into the living room, rolling her eyes as she went.

"Who's Brenda?" Elaine said, running her hand along the spines of the cactus.

"One of your mother's friends from OA."

"I give up," Elaine said. Her fingertips were bleeding; she put them in her mouth.

"Overeaters Anonymous. Your mother can be on the

phone day and night with those people. If any of them feel like they're about to go stuff their faces with a nice Sara Lee cake, for example, they call someone in this network they've got set up and talk their heads off instead of finishing the cake. Mommy lost fifteen pounds, by the way. Looks great, doesn't she?"

"Terrific." Elaine turned around in her chair so she could see her mother. "Wonderful," she said.

"You, on the other hand—"

"I'm fine."

"Feel like talking your head off to your old father?"

"About what?"

"Whatever. How about what you're going to do to get the boys back."

"This is the last time I'm going to repeat this," Elaine said, "so pay attention: they're perfectly happy where they are. Perfectly."

"They can't be. Children belong with their mother. That's the way it works in this world."

"It seems to me I've heard that before—twice yesterday and once the day before that."

"Does it sound any better today?"

"Worse," Elaine said.

Her mother came back out onto the terrace, eating the largest carrot Elaine had ever seen, and she was reminded of Jesse and Matthew, aged three and five, dressed in their Popeye pajamas, holding carrots in their hands as they sat on their knees in front of the television set watching some dopey program—"Gilligan's Island," she thought it was. They were young enough then that their heads smelled sweet when she bent to kiss them. She hadn't noticed when the sweetness disappeared; one day, it was simply gone.

She couldn't explain why her children had done what they had. The morning after she and Peter had driven home from the city, they had just finished breakfast and Jesse and Matthew were about to leave the table when Peter said, "Sit still a minute." They listened to him talk, staying silent until Peter said it was all up to them, whatever they wanted to do was fine. "Think carefully. Take your time," Elaine started to warn them, but already Matthew was saying he would stay with his father and Jesse was nodding his head up and down, saying that was what he wanted, too. They shrugged their shoulders when she questioned them, and she didn't have the heart to press the issue. If they had been daughters, it might have been different; she just didn't know.

After she left, she settled herself into an apartment in Fort Lee and found a job as a secretary in a private school in Manhattan—the first job she'd ever had. She stayed away from the house in Fair Lawn and talked to Peter briefly now and then. She spoke to Matthew and Jesse only once; she was near tears throughout the conversation and couldn't wait to hang up. They talked about school—book reports, and new gym uniforms, and the science teacher who made Matthew come in at the end of the day and stare at the clock on the wall for half an hour as punishment for talking in class. The boys talked easily, as if it had been hours rather than months that had passed since they heard her voice. At the end, she told them she missed them, then hung up before she could hear their response.

It was spring vacation and she was ready to see them, finally; to see what would happen. She wouldn't expect too much of them—if they were stiff as strangers at first, she was prepared to draw back and let them approach her at their own pace. Maybe, after their week together in Florida was up, they would decide to see each other every weekend, or every other weekend. Beyond that, she couldn't speculate. She certainly wasn't about to ask them to come and live with her, to set herself up for being kicked in the teeth again. That was what it had felt like this winter—a swift hard blow that left her so weak she could hardly move.

Her parents kept wanting to know what she had done. It's easy enough to be a lousy mother, her mother told her. You think you're doing everything right and then one day it turns out you were all wrong.

Elaine knew what her mother had done wrong. She had been a mother who couldn't wait for her children to grow up. Elaine and Philip, her younger brother, were always treated like adults; whenever there was trouble, they were expected to act calmly and reason things out. Once, at the train station, when they were on their way to the city to see *My Fair Lady,* Philip, who was terrified of escalators, couldn't bring himself to put one foot in front of the other and step onto the moving stair. "Just get a grip on yourself," their mother had shouted, while Elaine, who was twelve, ran down the other escalator to Philip and took his hand. It was the middle of the winter, but Philip's hand was moist and warm. Elaine promised him that it didn't matter whether they ever got to the city to see *My Fair Lady* that day, she only wanted him to stop crying. After the train left without them, their mother came down from the platform. "Get away from him," she said to Elaine. "I don't want you feeling sorry for him. The whole world knows how to deal with escalators. What's so special about him?" Elaine watched her brother lick tears from the corners of his mouth, and she wanted to lift him off the ground and fly him high above the escalator all the way to the city, leaving her mother behind with a look of absolute astonishment on her face. But Philip finally made it up the escalator and was forgiven. It was her mother who was never forgiven—not by Elaine, anyway.

"Do I care that Brenda has to put her mother into a nursing home?" her father was saying. "Does Elaine care?"

"What?" Elaine said.

"Tell your mother you couldn't care less."

"All right, I get the picture," her mother said.

"Can't we talk about something pleasant for a change?"

"What should we talk about? The weather? Even that kind of talk gets me in trouble."

"Talk to your daughter. Find out what's on her mind."

"I'm going to take a nap," Elaine said. "That's what's on my mind."

"Are you tired?" her mother said. "I'm not surprised. A long day of shopping can be very exhausting."

"I'm a people-watcher," Elaine's mother announced in the airport coffee shop the following afternoon. During breakfast they'd got a call from Peter saying the boys would be arriving at three fifty-five. After the call, Elaine had gone alone to the beach in Fort Lauderdale, taken a quick swim, then slept in the sun for an hour and returned to the apartment feeling fairly self-possessed. (It was the one time she'd been away from both her parents—the one time she'd successfully avoided them.) Now it was almost three thirty, and she was close to panic.

"People fascinate me. I could look at them for hours," her mother went on. "Look at the couple over there." She motioned toward a man with a cowboy hat and a big red mustache, and the black woman who sat opposite him. Their baby was asleep in a plastic infant seat they had placed on the table. "Now, what do you think motivates people like that?"

"What do you think motivates your mother?" Elaine's father asked. He smiled at her. "Plain old-fashioned nosiness?"

Elaine smiled back, but her hand shook as she reached for her water glass.

"Go ahead and laugh," her mother said. "I guarantee you ninety-nine percent of the people in this world would understand my point."

"I think," her father said, "the time has come for me to make my speech."

"If it's the one about mothers and children and who belongs with whom, you can cancel it," Elaine said.

"Give me a chance," her father said. "I just want to give you a little piece of advice, that's all. You listen to what I'm going to say to you and you'll have those children eating out of the palm of your hand one-two-three."

"Excuse me," Elaine said, and pushed back her chair.

"You can't afford to make any more mistakes, Lainie Bug," her father called after her as she headed for the rest rooms at the back of the coffee shop.

Inside, she rushed past a teenage girl who was tweezing her eyebrows in front of a large mirror over a row of sinks. She locked herself into a stall, dropped the seat cover, and sat down at the very edge. She closed her eyes. The stall reeked of strawberry-scented air freshener; still, it was easier to breathe now that she was alone.

In the dark she told herself who she was: a grown woman scared to death of two little boys. Her own children. She had always wanted to be a mother, had always wanted babies. You couldn't go wrong with babies; there was no possibility of disappointment. You could hold them as close as you needed to, tell them all day long how much you loved them, and never feel foolish.

One night last summer, already suspecting her marriage was lost, Elaine had led the boys into her darkened bedroom, and in their pajamas Jesse and Matthew stretched themselves out on the floor and stared in amazement at the hundred glow-in-the-dark stars and planets she had stuck on her ceiling that afternoon—a whole galaxy that shimmered endlessly above them. Peter was away in Japan on a business trip, on the other side of the world; there was no one to question what she had done with her day. After the boys were settled, Elaine got down on the floor, concentrating on nothing except the perfect faces of her children. When she awoke two hours later, her neck was stiff and the boys were gone. There was a light summer blanket covering her; someone, Jesse or Matthew, or maybe both of them, had bent over her while she slept.

"We thought you fell in and drowned," her father said when Elaine made her way back to the table. "Like that time at the World's Fair when you and your friend what's-her-name disappeared into the bathroom for a nice relaxing smoke. I couldn't imagine what you two were doing in there for so long. Of course, as soon as I got a whiff of you I knew what it was all about.''

"You all right?" her mother said. She touched her lips to Elaine's forehead. "Nice and cool."

"Do you want a Coke or something?" her father said.

"Not me," Elaine said. "We really should get a move on. I don't even know why I sat down again."

They got to the gate just as the first passengers from Newark appeared. Matthew and Jesse were right up front, dressed identically in tweed jackets, tan pants with cuffs, and Weejuns. Jesse was wearing glasses and had a flesh-colored patch over his right eye. Elaine ran to him. "What's the matter with your eye? When did you start wearing glasses?" she said. She kissed him and then she kissed Matthew. Neither of them kissed her back, though Jesse hugged her and Matthew shook her hand.

"Can't you give your mother a kiss?" her mother said.

"I'm in seventh grade," Matthew said. "I shake hands."

"And what about your brother?"

"Me?" Jesse said. "I hug, but I don't kiss."

Elaine said, "What's the patch for? Tell me what's wrong." She sat down in a padded chair opposite the check-in counter. Everyone else stood around her.

"It's just a lazy eye," Jesse said cheerfully. "It won't do any work unless I force it to. With a patch over the other eye, the lazy eye has to do all the work. You understand what I'm saying?"

"Why didn't your father tell me?" Elaine said. "Why didn't you tell me?"

"He says 'Hi,'" Matthew said. "I forgot all about it."

"You know what? His girlfriend bought us Star Wars costumes, even though it wasn't Halloween," Jesse said.

"God, what a jerk." Matthew put his hand over his brother's mouth.

"It's all right." Leaning forward, Elaine took Matthew's hand away from Jesse and held it. "Your father can have as many girlfriends as he wants. It makes no difference to me whatsoever."

"Well, he doesn't have one anymore. She dumped him."

Jesse said, "She used to make breakfast for us a lot on Saturdays and Sundays. She'd be there real early in the morning, like seven o'clock. She was a real early bird, Dad said."

"This kid is unbelievable," Matthew said.

Quickly Elaine's mother said, "Who would like to go for a midnight swim tonight? The water will be nice and warm, and we'll have the whole pool to ourselves."

"If it's really summertime here, can we have a barbecue?" Jesse asked.

"Sorry, guys," her father said. "No barbecuing allowed. Those are the rules of the condominium."

Jesse tried again. "Instead of a barbecue, can we go to Disney World?"

"You don't want to go to Disney World," her father said. "It's a four-hour drive each way. And you've already been to Disneyland, haven't you?"

"Are we going to have fun on this trip, or what?" Matthew said. "What did we come down here for?"

"What do you mean? You came down here to be with your mother," Elaine's mother said. "That's the main thing."

Elaine studied her shoes, yellow espadrilles that she had bought just for the trip. The little toe on each foot had already worn holes through the canvas, she noticed. When she looked up, Jesse was dancing, shifting his weight back and forth from one foot to the other, his arms in the air, his elbows and wrists bent at right angles. Some sort of Egyptian dance, Elaine thought.

"Look at me. I'm Steve Martin," Jesse yelled. " 'Born in Arizona, moved to Babylonia. King Tut.' "

"Terrific," Elaine said, and clapped her hands.

"Oh, Jesus," Matthew said.

·     ·     ·

Ignoring her mother's warning and her father's dire predictions, Elaine took the boys everywhere they wanted to go: Monkey Jungle, Parrot Jungle, and the Seaquarium. The boys seemed excited and happy, though often they would run ahead of her, too impatient to stay by her side. Once, from a distance, Elaine saw Jesse casually rest his arm on his brother's shoulder as the two of them stood watching a pair of orangutans groom each other; she kept waiting for Matthew to shake Jesse off, but it never happened. Two nights in a row, they went to see the movie *Airplane!* A couple of nights, they played miniature golf. At the end of each day, Jesse and Matthew told Elaine they had had "the best time." She supposed that this meant the trip was a success, that they would have nothing to complain about to their father when they went back home. She had kept them entertained, which was all they seemed to have wanted from her. She might have been anyone —a camp counselor, a teacher leading them on class trips, a friend of the family put in charge while their parents were on vacation. There was plenty of time to talk, and they told her a lot—long involved stories about the fight Jesse had recently had with his best friend, the rock concert Matthew had gone to with two thirteen-year-olds, the pair of Siamese fighting fish with beautiful flowing fins they'd bought for the new fish tank in their bedroom—all about the things that had happened to them in the four months they had been out of touch. But she still didn't know if they were really all right, if they loved their father, loved her. You couldn't ask questions like that. When, several years ago, her brother had started seeing a shrink, he'd complained that his parents were always asking him if he was happy. It's none of their business, the shrink told him—if you don't feel you want to give them an answer, don't. As simple as that.

It was nearly midnight; the boys had just gone to bed. Elaine went into her parents' room, where her mother and father were sitting up in their king-size bed watching "Columbo" on a small color TV. Dick Van Dyke was tying his wife to a chair.

He took two Polaroid pictures of her and then he picked up a gun. His wife insisted he was never going to get away with it; he aimed the gun at her and pulled the trigger.

"Wait a minute," Elaine's mother said. "Is this the one where Columbo tricks him into identifying his camera at the—"

"Thanks a lot," her father said. "You know how I love Peter Falk."

"Who knows, maybe I'm wrong."

"You're not," Elaine said. "I saw this one, too."

"Well, it's nice to be right about something."

Elaine lay down on her stomach at the foot of the bed, facing the TV set. She yawned and said, "Excuse me."

"All that running around," her mother said. "Who wouldn't be tired?"

"It's not necessary to run like that all day long," her father said. "Didn't those two kids ever hear of sleeping around the pool, or picking up a book or a newspaper? Maybe they're hyperactive or something."

"They're kids on vacation. What do they want to read the newspaper for?" her mother said.

Elaine sat up and swung her legs over the side of the bed. "It's my fault," she said. "I couldn't bring myself to say no to them about anything."

"Did you accomplish anything all those hours you were running?" her mother asked. "Do you feel like you made any headway?"

Elaine was watching an overweight woman on TV dance the cha-cha with her cat along a shining kitchen floor. "What?" she said.

"Of course, if they really are just fine there with Peter and his sleep-over girlfriends, that's another story," her father said.

"Quiet," her mother said. "Look who's here."

Jesse stood in the doorway, blinking his eyes. "There's a funny noise in my ears that keeps waking me up," he said. He sat down on the floor next to the bed and put his head in Elaine's lap. "You know," he said, "like someone's whistling in there."

Elaine hesitated, then kissed each ear. "Better?"

"A little."

"More kisses?"

Jesse shook his head.

"Let me take you back to bed." Elaine walked him to the little den at the other end of the apartment, where Matthew was asleep on his side of the convertible couch. Jesse got onto the bed. On his knees, he sat up and looked out the window. "I can't go to sleep right now," he said quietly. Beneath them, the water was black; above, the palest of moons appeared to drift by. There were clouds everywhere, and just a few dim stars.

"Did you want to tell me something?" Elaine waited; she focused on the sign lit up on top of the Holiday Inn across the Waterway.

"We're getting a new car. A silver BMW," Jesse said dreamily. "We saw it in the showroom." He moved away from the window and slipped down on the bed. "We might drive it over to Fort Lee and come and see you. And when Matthew has his license, the two of us will pick you up every day and take you anywhere you want to go."

Elaine still faced the window; she did not turn around. "To the moon," she said. "Will you do that for me?"

Jesse didn't answer for a long time. "We can do that," he said finally, and when she turned to look at him he was asleep.

# California

*H*e was already living in his new apartment when he met Margo. It was summer. His divorce, after twenty-nine years of marriage, had recently become final, and Jack didn't know what to do with himself. He signed up for a film course at the New School called Psychoanalysis Views Contemporary Cinema, mostly because his friends kept saying it was important for him to get out of the house, and it seemed like good advice. The class met Thursday nights at eight and for the first meeting he bought a package of ball-point pens and dressed up in a blazer and expensive loafers he had carefully chosen from his closet. At the end of the lecture, a narrow-faced girl with pretty red hair who had been sitting in front of him turned around and asked if she could borrow some change for a phone call. He gave it to her, collected his legal pad and pens, and followed her out of the room. He tried to eavesdrop after she got into the phone booth, but it was noisy in the hallway and he couldn't hear much. The girl was tall, in her late twenties, he guessed, and she was dressed like a college boy, in tan pants, Top-Siders, and a green shirt with a little alligator on it. He watched as she slammed the receiver down and shook her head.

"Idiot," she said, when she came out of the booth.

"Who?" said Jack.

"The man I live with."

"I see."

"Don't look so sad," said the girl, and laughed. Then she told him her name was Margo and that she was going to get something to drink at the snack bar before she went home. "You can come with me, if you want to," she said. "I'll break a dollar and get the money I owe you."

He was surprised to learn at the snack bar that she was only twenty-one and had just graduated from Dartmouth. She wanted to go to law school, but not now. All she wanted now was a job that paid two hundred dollars a week and wouldn't be too much of a strain. "I'm a very good typist," she said. "Seventy-five words a minute. What about in your office? Do you know if they're looking for anyone?"

"I'm retired now," Jack told her.

"You're kidding."

Jack laughed. "I bet you were fooled because I've got such a great head of hair." His hair was dark and thick, something he had always been proud of. And he was in good shape for sixty-two, he thought, except for the sallow circles that had settled under his eyes just before his divorce. He wanted Margo to know that a couple of times women had told him he looked like he might have been James Garner's older brother, but he couldn't think of a graceful way to work it into the conversation.

"What does a retired person do all day?" said Margo.

"Go to the library. Play racquetball in the school yard in my neighborhood. Walk the streets."

"And what about your wife?"

"What about her?"

"Are there any jobs in her office?"

"I lost her," said Jack. Usually he spoke too loudly, and he was used to people telling him to keep his voice down. Now he was almost whispering. "She was taken from me about a year ago."

"Oh," said Margo, and looked directly into his face. "I'm very sorry."

"It was an extraordinary marriage," said Jack. "We were inseparable. In all the time we were married we never spent a single night apart." He had lied to Margo, and now he couldn't stop. He went on talking, not knowing how he was going to end his story. It had to be Louise's fault, he thought, for divorcing him and making him desperate for a young girl's sympathy.

The truth was that he had been married to a woman who ran away from home several times a year, disappearing on short, mysterious trips that always took him by surprise. She would pack a flight bag and slip out without ceremony, leaving a note saying she expected to be back in a couple of days. One time, toward the end of their marriage, Louise was gone for almost two weeks, and Jack was frantic. He made a lot of phone calls that got him nowhere. Then, as a last resort, he called her psychiatrist and found out, at least, that she was safe.

He heard himself telling Margo that the very worst time had been after the funeral, when he had packed Louise's clothing into shopping bags and taken it to the Salvation Army. Finally he stopped talking, breaking off in the middle of a sentence. He was silent for a moment, and then he said, "I'm a crazy old man tonight. The truth is that my wife divorced me. But it wasn't because she didn't love me. It was her goddamn shrink who destroyed our marriage. He kept telling her our relationship wasn't worth saving, until one day she finally believed it."

Margo took the thin tortoiseshell headband from her hair and put one end of it into her mouth. She bit it so hard they both heard it crack.

"Look what I did," said Jack. "I made you so nervous you're eating plastic."

"I have to go home now," said Margo. "Why don't you give me your phone number." She got out a pen and wrote his name and number down on the back of her hand.

· · ·

Four nights later, just after dinner, Jack's doorbell rang. He ran from the kitchen, his hands dripping dishwater. He wiped them on his pants and slid back the bolt. Margo stood facing him across the foyer of the apartment.

"I lost your phone number," she said. "I took a shower and accidentally washed it off my hand. Then when I looked you up in the book and saw your address, I decided to take a walk over here."

He was surprised at how pretty she looked. Her hair was pulled back from her face with two small barrettes, and she was dressed in a white skirt and a thin flowered blouse that he could see through if he tried hard enough.

"You know, you were wearing boys' clothes the last time I saw you," he said. "You look wonderful now."

Margo smiled. "Actually, I came by to give you something." She handed him a bracelet of pale, shiny balls.

"I wouldn't be caught dead wearing jewelry, but thank you anyway."

"It's not jewelry," said Margo. "They're worry beads." She took a piece of paper out of her pocket and read from it. " 'Guaranteed to prevent heart attacks, suicide, divorces, and cigarette smoking. When troubled or lonely the beads will ease even your worst anxiety.' "

"Obviously I'd be a fool not to keep them," Jack said.

"A friend sent them to me from Greece. I thought you might want to have them in the house. Just in case." Margo walked into the middle of the living room and turned slowly in a small circle. The room was empty except for a couch and a desk and several bookcases.

"I love the brick wall and the high ceilings," Margo said. "You could use a little more furniture, though. Don't you even have a table to eat at?"

"I eat at my desk over by the window. It reminds me of my days at the office."

"You let your wife keep all the furniture?"

"I'm not a petty man," said Jack. "I don't waste my time fighting over little things."

"Where's your wife? Does she still live in New York?"

"You certainly ask a goddamn lot of questions."

"You shouldn't insult a person who's brought you a gift."

"Okay. My wife lives on Riverside Drive. She teaches at City College. She has a PhD."

"That's it?"

"What else do you want me to tell you?" He stared off into a corner of the room. His voice grew soft. "She's very small and quiet, and likes keeping to herself. She hates going out—whenever we were invited anywhere it was a battle to get her dressed and out the door of our apartment. When she came home from school all she wanted to do was lie in bed and read her scholarly journals. She didn't even like me to talk to her very much. But she needed to know I was close by. I stayed home and crept around the place, trying not to disturb her."

Margo touched him on the cheek, so delicately he wondered if he had imagined it. Her hair skimmed the top of his shoulder. He wasn't afraid to kiss her. The sound of people fighting over a parking space drifted up from the street below, and Margo sighed and pushed his arms away.

"Where are you going?" he said anxiously, but she had only gone to close the window.


It was a long white windowless room, and except for the sound of balls being hit in courts nearby, it was easy to pretend they were entirely alone and inapproachable, deep within their own secret shelter. Twice a week that summer they played racquetball in the basement court Margo had found. Later Jack would insist that this was where he had fallen in love with her, in an empty white room that smelled of sweat.

He had never had anyone so devoted to him, so eager to share things with him. On days that they happened not to see each other, Margo called him often, to read him a passage from a book she was in the middle of, to remind him there was a program on TV he ought to watch, or just to say that she felt like hearing his voice. Sometimes when they were out together, he'd drop her off at her apartment and return home to find something in the mailbox from her, a photograph of herself as a little girl that she wanted him to have, and once a handful of miniature purple flowers she had dried and gathered together in a rubber band.

He kept everything she gave him and stored it all in a special accordion folder he had marked with her name. One day he would put the folder into his vault at the bank, next to the stacks of silver dollars his father had left him when he died.

"No one's ever loved me like that girl does. She'd do anything for me," he told Louise over the phone in the fall. He and Margo had been together four months. He was sure he no longer mourned his marriage, and he didn't mind talking to Louise at all. He even found he looked forward to her occasional calls.

"I'm delighted that you're so happy," said Louise.

He wanted to tell her it was the happiest he'd ever been, but he thought Louise might be insulted. "I never expected something wonderful could happen to me in my old age," he said.

"What does her boyfriend have to say about all this?" said Louise.

"She got rid of him. She told him about me one day and a few days later he was gone. One two three. Just like that."

"Good for you."

"Are *you* all right? Forgive me for not asking you sooner."

"Dr. Schonfeld says I'm suffering from low self-esteem."

"You have a PhD. How could anyone with a PhD have low self-esteem?"

"Tell me about your girlfriend. Are you going to marry her?"

"Never. I'm just going to enjoy it while I can."

"Why?" said Louise. "Why shouldn't you marry the girl who'd do anything for you?"

"You have a high IQ," said Jack. "Figure it out." Louise was silent for so long he grew impatient. "You must be out of your mind if you think that a girl like that could live happily ever after with an old man like me."

They had planned to spend the entire weekend together, and Margo had arrived at Jack's apartment on Friday night with a canvas book bag tightly packed with clothing. It was on Saturday, as they were wandering through Central Park, that she admitted she'd been thinking about moving in with him. But the idea of sharing an apartment with her frightened Jack: there were too many things that could go wrong, and he didn't want to risk it. "Living with an old man on a day-to-day basis isn't the easiest thing in the world," he told her. "Anyway, I'm just not sure it would be the best thing for you to do right now. Maybe later, in a couple of months, we can start thinking about it again."

"I can get along fine on my own," said Margo. "But why shouldn't I be with you all the time if that's what I want? You still don't believe it's possible for two people to live together happily, do you? You think that because you and your wife couldn't handle it . . ."

"No," said Jack, "you're wrong. It doesn't have anything to do with my wife at all.".

"Okay," said Margo, but her shoulders drooped. "I'm not about to force myself on anyone. I'll just try you again when you've wised up."

He looked at her face to make sure she wasn't angry, and was relieved when she let him take her hand. It was a remarkably clear day near the end of October, and the trees all through the park had recently turned their colors. They approached Bethesda Fountain and then walked on toward the lake beyond it, which was crowded with people in slow-moving rowboats. When Jack said he didn't want to walk anymore, they stopped along the shoreline and ate from a small bag of apples Margo had brought with her. They were both wearing dungarees and Dartmouth sweat shirts. Jack's sweat shirt was a gift from Margo. A friend had helped get her a job in a law office on Park Avenue, and every payday she seemed to be buying Jack another gift; classical records that all sounded the same to him, and small, expensive books of modern poetry by people he had never heard of. He didn't tell her that listening to classical music always depressed him, and that the poetry she liked so much seemed deliberately obscure.

In most respects he thought of her as tough, a "hustler," he called it, someone who would always be able to take care of herself. (When he considered this, it became clear to him how very much alike he and Margo were.) She had mentioned her family only once, to say that they had never felt able to depend on each other for much. He knew she had fooled around with drugs and men a lot when she first got to college. He found himself admiring her for being adventuresome.

In the park now, Margo stood up and aimed an apple core into a garbage can. Then she dropped down onto the grass and leaned back on her elbows. "I started working on the essays for my law school applications last night," she said.

It was something they didn't talk about. He knew that she was applying to Columbia and NYU and several schools in California. Sometimes at night he dreamed of her going to school, sharing classes with hundreds of boys her own age, and he woke up in a cold sweat. He had to change into fresh pajamas and lay a towel over the damp sheets before he could fall asleep again. The only thing that could calm him then was the bottle of Valium Louise had let him have when he moved out of the apartment.

"Good for you," he said now to Margo. "I'm sure it's a smart idea to get the applications out as soon as you can."

"It's going to be hard," said Margo. "I'll be working all the time. You'll have to be patient with me."

He saw himself bringing her endless cups of coffee late at night, and tenderly rubbing the back of her neck for her when she had been studying too long. And certainly he would be smart enough to know when to stay out of her way. He would get used to the rhythm of her work and plan his days accordingly. He might even go through some of her casebooks so he could respond intelligently when she talked about her courses.

"If you went to NYU maybe we could look for an apartment in the Village," he said, just to see how she would react.

"Or if I end up in California, you'll come out there with me. You could take up jogging and skateboarding and stay out in the sun all day."

"New York is the greatest city in the world," said Jack. "I've lived here all my life. And that's where I want to die, not in California."

"I'm not going to listen to you if you're going to talk like that," said Margo, and put her hands over her ears.


They had their lunch not far from the Seventy-second Street entrance to the park, alongside a small shallow creek, where, Margo said, in the summertime long ago she'd searched for killies with a butterfly net. After they finished eating Jack lay with his head on Margo's stomach. A squirrel scuttled past, dragging a turquoise tissue from its mouth. Margo played with his hair, running a twig through it gently. The sun was shining in his face. His eyes were closed, and he was beginning to feel drowsy.

"Why is it that you never had children?" said Margo.

"It just would have been a terrible mistake," he said.

"Did you ever feel bad about it?"

"I don't think so, but it's hard to remember."

"You could have a child with me," said Margo.

"Absolutely not." That she had real faith in their future together touched him immeasurably, but he had to set her straight before she got carried away. "No one's getting married and no one's having any babies. You're going to school next year. I'll probably be out of the picture before you know it." His heart was beating very quickly. He could see through to the end of their affair, and the boy who would take Margo away from him: a self-confident kid in a gray three-piece suit and gleaming cordovan shoes.

"Why would I want you out of the picture?" said Margo.

"It's common sense."

"Who told you that? Where do you get your information from?"

He lifted his head from her stomach. He felt a little dizzy. "Do you think I'm wrong?" he said.

"It's probably the first time I've ever been in love with anyone," Margo said. "Why can't you let me enjoy it?"


They were supposed to go out for dinner that night, but Margo didn't feel well. She was lying on Jack's bed, barefoot, kneading her toes into the mattress. "You have to go to a drugstore and get me a heating pad," she said.

"Since when is a heating pad good for a stomachache?"

"It's not a stomachache," said Margo. "It's cramps."

He tried to turn up the sides of the bedspread and cover her, but she yelled at him to leave her alone. When he got back from the drugstore with the heating pad, she was on the floor in the living room, rocking from one hip to the other. He found an outlet and plugged in the cord.

"What would I do without you?" said Margo.

"I'm the glue that holds you together, right?"

Margo didn't answer. She closed one hand into a fist and scraped her teeth against her knuckles. The cord from the heating pad had gotten twisted around her thigh. Jack bent down to untangle it.

"Don't hover over me like that," said Margo. "Please."

"Tea," he said. "How about if I make you some tea?" Not waiting for an answer, he went into the kitchen. The cabinets were mostly empty, but on the window ledge he found a box of Celestial Seasonings Pelican Punch. There was a picture on the front of some animals identified as Rupert Pelican, PhD, and Pumble Platypus. He waited silently for the water to boil and then brought the tea out to Margo. "It's got blackberry leaves, coconut, and almond in it," he said. "What do you think?"

She sat up slowly, holding the heating pad to her stomach, as Jack lifted the cup to her lips. "You're so good," she said. "No one's ever been quite this good to me."

He went back to the kitchen and returned with the box of tea. He read Margo the children's story printed on the side panel. It was all about Rupert Pelican's birthday party. He read it in a voice that would make her laugh. She really was beginning to feel a little better, she said, as she stretched herself out on the floor on her stomach again.

"Wouldn't you rather lie down in the bedroom?" he asked.

"If you'll stay in there with me."

When he got onto the bed beside her, he suddenly felt tired, and he was asleep before Margo was. Once during the night he awoke to find that he had been kissing her. He eased himself to his side of the bed and struggled to make out what time it was on the digital clock. He saw a three and two zeros. "Three hundred," he murmured, but it didn't sound right to him, and he fell back to sleep trying to figure it out.


The one secret he kept from her was his age. "What does it matter?" Jack said when she wanted to know exactly how old he was. "What difference does it make? You can see that at the very least I'm old enough to be a close relative of yours we won't mention by name. What more do you need to know than that?"

That Sunday afternoon she tried to trick him. They were on their way back from the Museum of Natural History, and had stopped off at the Christian Science Reading Room on Fifth Avenue because Jack wanted to rest. "Think of all the people who were alive when you were young," Margo said when they sat down. "Freud, D. H. Lawrence, Tolstoy. Isn't it amazing?"

"Tolstoy," said Jack in his loudest voice. "That was the nineteenth century. What's the matter with you?"

Suddenly there was a middle-aged woman standing over them. "If you're not going to read our literature you'll have to leave," she said.

"Tolstoy died in 1910," said Margo, when they were out on the street again.

"Definitely before my time."

"How much before?"

"End of conversation," said Jack.

They didn't discuss his age again. Eventually Margo confessed that she had gone through his wallet one night while he was sleeping, and had gotten the information she wanted from his driver's license.


At Christmas Margo flew to San Diego to visit her older sister Caroline, and Jack restrained himself from calling her until she had been gone for forty-eight hours. He put on a recording of the Brandenburg concertos she had given him, and then made the call. "You hear your friend Bach there in the background?" he said, but she was already talking about how wonderful California was. There were grapefruit and orange orchards in her sister's yard, she told him. And mountains that could be seen from the windows at the back of the house. She was learning to skateboard. Tomorrow she and Caroline were driving down to Mexico for the day. As she talked Jack stared out his kitchen window, which overlooked an alleyway and was covered with soot. He didn't like to think of Margo in a distant place where mountains could be seen from the window.

He wanted her back in New York, on familiar ground.

"Listen," he said. "Put your sister on. I have to talk to her."

When Caroline picked up the phone he said, "Tell me how she is. Is she all right?"

"She's great. We're having a terrific time together."

"Tell her not to go too fast when she's on that skateboard," he said. "She could break an arm if she's not careful."

"Why don't you tell her yourself?"

"Not me," said Jack. "I'm not her mother. Or her father."

"More power to you," said Caroline.

He could hear her saying something to Margo, and then laughter.

"Just keep her away from all that cocaine you people are so fond of out there," he said, but she had already hung up.

The phone call left him feeling he couldn't sit still. He shut off the stereo and started to get some clothing ready to bring to the laundromat down the street. He separated everything into two piles, dark and light. By the time he was finished, he had lost interest in the project. He left the laundry on the floor in his bedroom and decided to call Louise. He knew she was probably home in bed, working her way through some magazines you never saw anyplace except the library.

She answered the phone on the ninth ring. "Where were you?" he asked.

"I couldn't decide whether I wanted to talk to anyone or not."

"Should I hang up?"

"Tell me how you are first. Where's your girlfriend tonight?"

"California. She'll be home in a week."

"So you'll be all alone on New Year's Eve. I'll have to remind myself to call you at midnight to wish you a happy New Year."

"Thanks." He hesitated. "Maybe you and I could go out somewhere that night."

"Why would I want to go to a restaurant and get myself depressed watching a lot of people trying frantically to have a good time?"

"You could come over here and we could have some champagne together."

"What are we celebrating?"

"You're right. Forget the whole thing. I just thought it would have been nice for both of us not to be alone."

"Don't be angry at me," said Louise. "I sent you a Christmas card last week. Did you get it?"

"No," said Jack. He knew she was lying.

"I sent it to you and your girlfriend. I thought you'd be pleased."

It occurred to him that she had never once seemed to be the least bit jealous of Margo. He couldn't understand how it was possible to be so dispassionate: he knew *he* wouldn't enjoy hearing about the men Louise was dating.

"Well, as long as you're not angry," she was saying. "I couldn't handle it if I thought someone was angry at me."

"No one's angry at you," Jack said.


Margo came to his apartment straight from the airport, looking sunburned and tired. He grabbed her as she walked in the door. He folded his arms around her back and kissed her hair. He had started growing a beard while she was away, and Margo rubbed her hand back and forth across his cheek without comment.

She wanted to know all the things he had done during the past week. He listed the museums he had wandered through and the Ross Macdonald books he had read one after the other. He didn't mention the hours he had spent sitting motionless in his living room brooding about her.

Margo sat down at his desk when he finished talking. "I'm a very honest person," she said. "There's something I did that I'm afraid to tell you about."

"I don't want to know anything about it," said Jack, and shut his eyes. He saw the Pacific in the background, and a blond, barefoot surfer filling her with beer on a deserted stretch of beach.

"If I had been thinking straight I wouldn't have done it."

"*Nobody* in California can think straight. You go out there and breathe the air and suddenly all your good sense is gone. I heard a joke about it in the supermarket last week. How many Californians does it take to change a light bulb?"

"How many?" said Margo, not sounding very interested.

"Four. One to change the light bulb and three to share the experience."

"Notice I'm not laughing."

"It's not funny. It's actually quite serious."

"I don't care," said Margo. "I loved it there. I wanted to stay there for the rest of my life."

"Feel free to do whatever you want."

Margo began to cry, soundlessly. Then, rubbing her eyes with her fists like a child, she let Jack lead her into the bedroom. He pulled down the shades and threw the clothes that were on the bed into the closet. "It's only eight o'clock California time," said Margo. "I'm not going to sleep. It's ridiculous."

"You're in New York," said Jack. "No one cares what time it is in California."

Margo sighed. "If I were there now, I could be relaxing in my sister's pool."

"Let's get this California business settled right now," said Jack. "You've already decided to go to school there, haven't you? I want to talk about it."

"Why don't we just wait and see how things go," said Margo.

"Because I'm too old to live my life like that."

"Well I'm not. Why should I spend my time worrying about what may or may not happen in the future?"

"You could at least try to be more patient."

"You're so afraid," said Margo. "You won't live with me or marry me because you're afraid it won't work. You won't come to California because you're afraid of leaving New York. And you're afraid that in New York I'll fall in love with some jerk at Columbia. What do you want? I don't think you know anymore."

Jack picked up the bracelet of worry beads from the night table next to him. He tossed them back and forth from one hand to the other. "You ought to go to sleep," he said finally. "Your eyes are all swollen from the sun. You look terrible."

He shut the door behind him. Then he went into the den, where there were piles of *National Geographic*s and a large, old-fashioned television set in a wooden cabinet. He turned on the TV to a public broadcasting station and switched off the lamp next to the couch. On the TV screen a very pregnant young girl was talking to an older woman. They were both sitting in swivel chairs and he understood that the girl was being interviewed.

"The day they told me I had leukemia," said the girl, "was my twenty-first birthday. Isn't that weird?" She smiled very shyly, and put her hair behind her ears.

"Could you tell me what you were thinking about while the doctors were talking to you?" said the interviewer. "Did you think they had made a mistake, that they had mixed you up with some other patient?"

The girl shook her head. "I just wanted to know whether I would make it to the baby's first birthday. It was the only thing that seemed important."

"And what did they tell you?"

"They said no, they didn't think so." There was a close-up of her face. Jack tried to concentrate on her ears, which were large and stuck out noticeably from her head.

The interviewer's face was impassive. "Do you feel as if you've been cheated?"

"Actually," said the girl, "I consider myself very lucky in the ways that really count. My marriage was the best thing that ever happened to me and—"

Jack got up and turned the sound off. The screen darkened and the people were gone. A one-line message appeared. It said the girl had died when her son was three months old. Then the interviewer was back in her swivel chair. She was talking to the girl's husband and parents. The baby was crawling around on the floor, while the family looked on, smiling.

"What are you smiling at?" said Jack. "What's the matter with you people?" he shouted.

"What?" said Margo. Her voice sounded faint from the other room.

He made his way over to her through the darkness. He looked for her face with his hands. Her skin felt very warm, and she moaned when he touched her. "You're not sick, are you?" he said.

"It's only sunburn," said Margo. "It stings a little, that's all."

He started to tell her about the girl he had seen on television. "She was your age and she had leukemia," he said, and then he couldn't talk anymore. He was close to tears; what was wrong with him? In his old age he was turning melancholy.

"So what happened to the girl?" said Margo.

"Who?"

"The girl with leukemia."

"She went into remission. It was a miracle," he said.

# Secrets

*T*here are four of us at the barbecue, two married couples. Eric, who is married to my younger sister, Lauren, and in charge of the chicken, accidentally tips a plateful of white meat into the grass. Eight pieces lie there, skin side down, and we stare at the patches of grass streaked red with barbecue sauce, all of us momentarily horrified and unable to move. Then Eric takes the garden hose and rinses each piece off delicately, with a fine spray of water.

Lauren frowns. She seems to be about to say something, but then walks off to the house. Her rubber thongs slap sharply against her feet. She is sweet-faced and small, and might almost be mistaken for a child. She unwittingly invites kisses on the forehead, pats on the cheek. People smile at her while she is speaking to them and often do not take the things she says seriously. I have seen it happen many times, seen her kept back by the illusion of innocence that surrounds her like a second skin. Although I don't radiate the particular charm that Lauren seems to, or affect people in quite the same way, I am also small and young-looking, and able to sympathize with her.

Eric takes Lauren seriously. They have been married for four years, nearly twice as long as William and I, and I have always understood them to be well matched in their tranquil, easy way. They live here in this rented house, in a small Vermont town, at a nice distance from their families. Eric is serene and soft-voiced. He designs and builds tables, chairs, and lamps, though most of his income is from his part-time job in a lumber store, where he sells two-by-fours and cans of varnish and paint, and dispenses advice to amateur craftsmen. He was once, in another life, a business major at Syracuse, a fact which I can hardly believe. The way Eric tells it, one night, despairing of the unimaginative, middle-class ordering of his life, he called his father and summoned him to a meeting. He booked a room for the two of them at a Holiday Inn and the following evening spent hours explaining why he was switching his major from business to forestry. Afterward, he and his father got amiably drunk on six cans of beer apiece and threw rolls of toilet paper and bedding into the snow outside their window, though the next morning at checkout time his father went back to Connecticut with, as he'd put it, "a heavy heart."

My husband and I live in New York City. William, who works for an advertising agency, is often restless and disappointed in his work, and he likes to hear Eric tell this story. Of all the people I care about deeply, William likes only Lauren and Eric. I believe this is because they are as determinedly rural as is possible for them. They carefully tend to their garden and show off their vegetables like new parents, discussing size and color and shape with great solemnity. They drive two and a half hours to the nearest movie and even farther to a department store. Several towns away there is candlepin bowling, which they play infrequently. And there is the one-room library where Lauren works.

Twice a week, Eric receives chemotherapy treatments for the small tumors that have appeared periodically on one leg and foot since the year before their marriage. He and my sister live with this uncertainty patiently, without rage, though I don't know if they have always been this way; I only know what I see on my visits.

Eric's father owns a chain of bath shops that sell expensive fixtures, towels, and shower curtains. He has a good deal of money, some of which he sends monthly to Lauren and Eric. At the beginning of their marriage, when the checks were uncomfortably large, Eric wrote emotional letters explaining why they would have to send them back. Soon his letters turned polite, and then they stopped altogether. Lauren and Eric put the checks in a special account from which they never draw, though they plan to someday buy land with it. Eric's illness has been woven into the fabric of their days. Except for the checks, their life together seems uncomplicated and untainted.

The barbecue is not going well. A sudden breeze blows smoke in Eric's eyes and he, too, retreats into the house, coughing and limping slightly, as if he had turned an ankle. William and I take over while he recovers from the smoke. From inside the house there is shouting. I am put off balance by the raised voices of people always so gentle.

When the chicken is finally done, we decide to bring it indoors and eat in the kitchen, away from the mosquitoes. We eat by candlelight, on dishes of assorted patterns, no two of which are the same. Lauren begins to apologize for the variety, but Eric says, "What are you apologizing for?" and quickly Lauren stumbles from the room, banging her chair against a cabinet door.

From the yard the singing of summer insects lulls us into an awkward peace. Lauren returns for dessert, without apology. Later, Eric and William go out to clean up the fireplace.

While Lauren washes the dishes we talk together. We have seen each other very little in the past few years, and so our talk is slow and shy. Lauren's guarding of secrets puzzles me, for I spill my life over to one friend and then another, carelessly giving myself away, revelation by revelation. But there has always been love between the two of us, a satisfying sympathy, a leftover from our easy, shared childhood.

When the dishes are washed, Lauren dries her hands on a towel that says "A Woman's Work Is Never Done." "Eric's father brought this up from one of the stores," she says, laughing. "It's hopeless." She pulls out a chair and sits down with me at the table.

I smile and sweep the crumbs that remain on the table into my palm.

She closes her eyes. "Eric isn't getting any better," she says. "The tumors come back so fast."

The candles on the table flicker; her face is golden, angelic. She is rocking back and forth in her chair, arms crossed against her stomach. Her eyes, open now, look sleepy, confused. I want her to tell me more than she has ever told anyone.

Lauren was a moody and secretive child. I remember walking by her room one summer night at bedtime and hearing her chanting: reciting numbers that seemed endless. I ran outside the house, stopping directly under her window, but the recitation was over. The shades were only partially down and I watched as Lauren, a tiny ghost in her faded nightgown, looked under her bed, checked inside the closet, and then counted the collection of china animals on the top of her dresser. Satisfied that all was in order, she at last got into bed. It was my first time spying, and though I could make little sense of what I had witnessed, what troubled me most was that this had been kept secret from me, that my sister's life was not open to me in the way I had always thought it to be. Even then, so many years ago, I did not believe in secrets.

William and I leave for New York the next day. Before breakfast, I write a note for Lauren on the back of a receipt from a gas station. The paper is thin and waxy and difficult to write on. The note says:

Dear L——
    I don't feel that I know very much, but I see that you're strong and patient.
    Things will go well.

I slouch mournfully in the passenger seat of our M.G. for nearly five hours as we drive homeward through Massachusetts and Connecticut. Occasionally, William tries to involve me in conversation; he talks about the new sports car he wants to buy, the house he wants to build, but I don't feel responsive to any talk of the future. In the car now a hard and sour lump of sorrow catches in my throat.

I see Lauren and Eric, shortly before their marriage, kissing outside the bathroom door in my parents' house. Lauren stands on her toes as her face meets Eric's, and the heels of her hard bare feet are blackened with dirt.

They did not care at all who caught them at it. Often Eric stood with his hands in the back pockets of Lauren's dungarees, or Lauren curled her toes around his ankles.


My mother and I are shopping together not long after my visit to Lauren's. We are impatient shoppers, losing interest quickly. Mostly it is an excuse for us to spend time with each other. I sit on the floor in my underwear in a department-store dressing room, rejected clothing all around me. My mother is seated on a small stool. She leans over and pulls the curtain tightly across the booth. She asks me if I am still happily married and sighs when I say I am. "I only like to hear about happy things," she says, but then we talk of Lauren.

"Your sister," says my mother, "was never a talker. It was always like pulling teeth, from the time she was a child. So now, in the midst of all this, who knows what she's thinking?" Her voice softens; the word *cancer* is uttered in a near-whisper, as if it were a sexual term mentioned in the presence of children—a word to be used with care. "Let me tell you something," she says. "No parent likes to see her child enter into a situation that's doomed from the start."

"Let's just wait and see what happens," I answer. "You might very well be wrong."

The carpeted floor is full of discarded straight pins, and, keeping my head lowered, I concentrate on arranging them in geometric patterns. I will not study my mother's sadness: the droop of her face, the eyes canine in sorrow.


Eric is in the hospital on Thanksgiving. He is sitting up in bed and smoking, his yellow beard full and strong against his narrow face. Partially draped by a sheet, his swollen left leg lies fiery and peeling, made monstrous by chemotherapy.

I look away, afraid of what more I might see out of the corner of my eye.

William and I give Eric a small display case filled with butterflies. He is pleased by it and props the case up in his lap. William discusses the butterflies with him, and the kinds of wood and varnish he used in making the case. It is a first creative effort and he is proud of it. They seem related by blood, these two lean, bearded men talking of butterflies in a hospital room. Afterward, William vomits at the curb where our car is parked.


The private manner in which my sister and her husband have chosen to live out the misery of his illness puzzles me. I hunger after the facts of their survival together. Though I know it is wrong of me, I call some of Lauren's friends, hoping for clarity. "Look," they say, one after another, "I don't know any more than you do." They are eager to discuss their own marriages, but I'm not interested in the interfering in-laws, the boredom, the complaints of selfishness that are detailed and digested in the blink of an eye. It's the complexity of my sister's troubles that I want to know about. Ignorant of details, I am of no use to her, of little comfort, hardly a sister at all.

In the years since Lauren's marriage, there's never been a baring of the soul, a revelation to me of true importance or consequence. She's kept me at a distance and I feel cheated, excluded. William says I ought to respect her silence, her need to keep her life to herself, but I believe that love entitles me to something more.

In the spring we visit them again. Eric is wearing specially made shoes now, the left heel of each pair extravagantly built up, a wedge of rubber meant to ease the disorder of a leg still swollen by the wonders of modern medicine. He uses a walking stick outdoors, looking as if he were seeking adventure as he greets us in the driveway.

Settling down in the living room, we all make much of how well everyone looks.

We decide to go canoeing. The four of us paddle across a wide and lovely lake and drift slowly under the sun. On the shore people are having a picnic, the cheerful sound of their activity reaching out across the lake, an arc of well-being that settles over us like something comfortable and familiar.

But soon Lauren and Eric are quarreling, mildly at first, about a doctor Lauren doesn't trust.

"Lay off, will you," Eric tells her after a while.

I drag my hand in the cool water and pretend that William and I are alone.

Lauren looks at Eric with exasperation. "You haven't the slightest notion of how to deal with these things," she says. "If it weren't for me, you'd be dead by now."

There is a splash and Eric is out of the boat, sidestroking slowly toward shore. The canoe hasn't tipped over, a small miracle.

That night, lying on a new and uncomfortable convertible sofa in my sister's living room, William and I whisper about our untroubled lives, anxious to separate ourselves from the misfortune that so clearly belongs not to us but to my sister and her husband. Good health and a comfortable marriage, these things that have always seemed unremarkable, so unworthy of contemplation, now suddenly appear to be a luxury.

But in the morning, when I see Lauren in a shabby pink terry-cloth robe setting the table for breakfast, adding a bowl of chrysanthemums in the center, I am shame-stricken for having last night taken comfort in my own life. I see exactly what it is I want: for Lauren to bring her life closer to mine, to share with me a substantial weight of grief that I can take with me when I leave. But I cannot ask her for any of it, nor can I console her in a weepy embrace, for it is not her way to allow these things. Instead, I ask her if I can help prepare breakfast, an offer she refuses.

One night in September I call them. Lauren answers the phone. She tells me that Eric has moved out, to live in a cabin at the edge of a nearby woods; that he quit his job at the lumber store and leads nature tours for the Parks Department.

I am stunned. In my mind, Lauren and Eric are poignantly bound by a threat of death that sets them apart from the rest of us. That they have failed to live peaceably together seems unforgivable, a terrible breach of love.

"It's all right," says Lauren, quick to fill the space of my silence. "Things are going to work themselves out. I'm happy alone, very comfortable." Her voice is animated, hopeful. She tells me that she saw Eric several weeks earlier. "I couldn't wait for him to leave," she says. "Everything he did annoyed me; he left cigarettes burning all over the house. What it is is that he's lost the ability to deal with practical matters."

"Well," I say, "it's not easy."

Lauren sighs and soon ends the conversation.

During the winter, Lauren comes to New York and we have lunch together. I learn that Eric has gone into remission, and deeper into the woods, an old young man with a walking stick venturing farther than I had guessed.

Lauren tells me she is living with a former high-school English teacher who breeds show dogs for a living now. She seems happy; her eyes glitter in the restaurant. That's all I know, for she will always be careful with her confidences.

# Still Life

*A*t his ex-in-laws' thirty-fifth wedding anniversary party, Brad is the only guest to arrive in faded corduroy pants and a sweater that has seen better days. All the men are in ties and jackets, and most of the women are wearing dresses and lots of jewelry. But in a crowd of fifty people, it is doubtful whether anyone will notice him, and, anyway, he's not planning to stay long. He's only here because Nina followed up a written invitation with a phone call begging him to come. Nina, his ex-wife, has a new husband and a new baby and is the happiest person she knows. When she told all this to Brad over the phone last week, he immediately fell silent, though he knew that she was waiting for him to congratulate her on having achieved with someone else what had been only a painful subject for discussion when she was married to him. Listening to her go on about her happiness had exasperated him, and he cut the conversation short, perhaps was even the slightest bit rude, telling her the toaster oven had just popped open with his dinner and that he couldn't talk anymore. To make up for his rudeness he bought her parents a pair of carved wooden candlesticks that cost him more than he'd intended to spend. And for the baby he settled on a bear dressed in a blue hooded coat, red rubber boots, and a broad-brimmed yellow felt hat. The bear came in three sizes; he quickly decided on the largest, wondering later just whom he'd been trying to impress.

When he was first married to Nina, Brad had done very well at the large corporate law firm he worked for. But working for what seemed to be a thousand hours a week on what he was sure were the most unworthy cases in the world made him miserable. Understanding this, Nina encouraged him to quit. Given a choice between misery and happiness, it would be crazy to make the wrong decision, she said.

They left the city and moved up the Hudson to a tiny rented house in Garrison so Brad could be a country lawyer with Nina working as his secretary in an office they shared at the front of the house, just off the kitchen. At lunchtime, they went into the living room and ate their sandwiches on a black vinyl couch while they laughed at ancient reruns of "I Love Lucy." The couch had been borrowed from Nina's parents, and it was the one where she and Brad made love every Saturday night before their wedding. Brad found himself remembering their whispered conversations and the time Nina had said she loved him, her voice so soft he hadn't caught the words. "You what?" he'd asked her more than once (probably sounding a little cranky), but Nina was too embarrassed to repeat it. Later, whenever one of them mentioned love, the other always answered, "You what?"

They'd been in Garrison almost a year when the transmission in their Toyota went, and their stereo system and TV set needed major repairs, all in the same month.

"I just can't live like this anymore," Nina said one afternoon in the office, laying her head down on the typewriter so that her mahogany-colored hair streamed over the edge of the desk dramatically. "It kills me to admit it, but I was brought up to want things." Her voice was apologetic, even embarrassed. None of the things she named seemed unreasonable: a house with rooms larger than closets; vacation trips to interesting places; and, most important, children.

When he came around to her and caught her hair in his hands, Brad could see that she was crying. "Our marriage," she said, lifting her face to look at him. "I can't imagine letting it go."

That night, in bed, they talked about Nina's wanting to have a child, both of them trying hard to see how a baby might fit comfortably into their life together, but they came to the same conclusion: there wasn't any way they could manage it in the near future.

"It's only a matter of being patient," he soothed her, "of waiting for things to fall into place." For Brad, what mattered most was that he loved his work, that he was actually providing a useful service to a handful of ordinary, honorable people.

The following year, which turned out to be the last year of their marriage, Nina had an accidental pregnancy which ended in early miscarriage. She insisted on showing Brad exactly what they had lost. Looking at a book of magnified photographs of an eight-week-old fetus with pudgy hands and fingers and an indistinct face, Brad felt nothing but confusion —the photographs were like a display of abstract paintings. He wasn't as patient with Nina as he ought to have been, he realized. He was disappointed in her for having all but given up on their small-town, small-time life (her words), for having convinced herself that neither of them was adventurous enough or romantic enough to live from hand to mouth with any degree of grace or pleasure.

He waited for her to leave him, and when she did he could make no sense of her explanation. She just didn't want to be married, she said, to a man who showed so few signs of ever being happy. Refusing to meet his eyes, she said, "I fantasize about some kind of happiness for you, but I can't figure out where it's going to come from."

"You're talking about yourself," Brad told her, staring at the little opal ring she twirled around her finger. "You're the one to whom everything looks imperfect, impossible."

· · ·

Now, nearly two years later, as he eases his way through Nina's parents' crowded living room and discovers Nina waving to him from a high-backed satin chair that looks like a throne, he has to smile. But his smile is vague, as if he were approaching someone he knew only slightly and couldn't remember from where.

"Didn't I get you that sweater for Christmas about a hundred years ago?" she asks him, but pleasantly.

He bends to kiss her, and as he does, the baby against her shoulder grabs a fistful of his hair and pulls so hard tears spring to Brad's eyes. Holding his breath, he unfolds the baby's tiny damp hand, saying, "Is this what they call love at first sight?"

"Don't feel special," Nina says, laughing. "She does that to just about everyone."

The baby, a little bald girl in a knitted white dress and white tights, looks at Brad with wide-open eyes and then yawns.

"It *is* kind of a boring party," Nina says. "Lots of fourth cousins I've probably seen twice in my life. I'm sorry Ken's not here. I think you guys might have been able to strike up a conversation or two." The baby hiccups. "Well, maybe not," Nina says. "Maybe it's just as well."

"He's at the hospital?"

"His beeper went off the minute we got here, and that was that."

"It must be hard, never knowing when your plans are going to be disrupted."

"Not so hard. You make the best of it, that's all."

"Unbelievable," Brad says. "Is that your new philosophy of life I'm hearing?"

"Baby doll," a voice says. "Brad!" He turns to see Nina's grandmother smiling in his direction. Approaching him, Evelyn puts a hand over each of his ears and kisses him on the forehead. "You know, I'm very disappointed in you," she says. "Come over here so I can talk to you." Leading him into a spare bedroom full of coats, she closes the door behind them and leans against a plastic-mesh playpen.

"I should have called you," Brad says. "I'm sorry I dropped out of sight like that."

"You know, when Nina told me she was going to marry this other young man, I just felt sick," says Evelyn. "It makes you sick to your stomach to hear a story like that. 'What's so terrible about Brad,' I asked her, 'that you couldn't make an effort to keep your marriage in one piece?' "

Nina's grandmother is five feet tall, but broad and fleshy. She is wearing black leather Space shoes, the only shoes that fit her at all, and a fancy silk dress with swirls of magenta and gray. "How do you like these new cataract glasses they've got me wearing?" she asks Brad. "They keep slipping down on my nose and all day long I'm annoyed with them."

"I didn't even know you'd had the surgery. Nina and I haven't really been in touch." He hangs his head, feeling bad that he's neglected her. When he was married to Nina, her grandmother used to send him a soft, battered-looking ten-dollar bill on his birthday, slipped between a large index card folded in half. Front and back, the index card said "With 'love' "—no signature. He and Nina had never figured out what the quotation marks meant, though near the end of their marriage, Nina admitted she'd always assumed her grandmother was mocking him, letting him know that in her eyes he would forever be an in-law, never the real thing. Brad, who was touched by her gifts (which he could never bring himself to spend), considered that ridiculous. There were four bills in all, one for each year of their marriage. He kept them in a coffee mug on the top of his dresser, along with some loose buttons, a set of tarnished cuff links, and a torch-shaped National Junior Honor Society pin that he'd given Nina as a joke when they'd got engaged.

"At the end of my life, I'm seeing things differently," Evelyn tells him. "I look through these dumb glasses and everything is bright and glittery, like diamonds." She says this with a mixture of amazement and disgust, shaking her head slowly. Now her voice has softened to a whisper. "Do you want me to tell you about Nina's new husband? I see things there that keep me up at night, if you understand what I'm saying."

Sitting at the edge of a bed piled with coats, Brad trails his hand through someone's mink. "She claims to be very happy," he says.

"For some people, women especially, the loneliness is too much. They'll do anything to avoid it," says Evelyn. She looks up at Brad, her eyes exaggerated and blurred behind the lenses of her glasses. "And you?"

"I work very hard," he says quickly, feeling defensive. "And after work, I'm usually in the basement, puttering around, refinishing furniture—that kind of thing." He stands up, sticks his hands in front of her face, lets her see that his fingers are stained a reddish brown.

Evelyn takes a step back from him. "So you're down in the basement all night. So that's what you've been up to."

"There's more," he says, but won't elaborate. There are friends he occasionally drinks with, women he occasionally sleeps with; there's no point in telling her any of this. Still, he hates it that his life sounds so stark, so needy. "I'm getting by," he says. "Sometimes it seems almost enough."

"This new husband," says Evelyn, "is a toothpick of a man. All sharp bones and about ten feet tall. Do you want to see a picture of him?"

"Are you kidding?" Brad says. "Not even a snapshot."

"He doesn't talk to her nicely. Even before they were married, he was speaking to her the wrong way, as if she were a salesgirl in some store wasting his time, showing him all the wrong things."

"Listen to me," Brad says. "You can't contradict someone when they say they're happy. It just can't be done."

"You stubborn mule," Evelyn says sadly. "I could just kill you. I could put my hands around your throat and . . ."


At Nina's suggestion, she and Brad are going to take the baby for a walk around the block in her carriage. Outside in front of the house, one of Nina's cousins is washing his new car, a Datsun 280ZX with a red leather interior. The cousin, who is called Bobby, is dressed in a zippered jump suit, despite the cold. Underneath a mimosa tree across from the Datsun is a portable tape deck playing David Bowie songs.

"Perfect day for a car wash," Bobby says, pointing to the cloudless sky with a dripping sponge.

"I just love your jump suit," Nina says. She winks at Brad. "Ideal for any occasion, no matter how formal."

"Did you get the invitation to my wedding?" Bobby asks.

"We're looking forward to it."

"Well, tear it up," says Bobby. "The wedding's off."

"That's a shame. I don't know what else to say."

"Yeah, well, to thine own self be true and all that jazz," Bobby says. "From now on, it's just me and my Z."

"Beautiful car," Brad says.

"You bet." Spinning around and facing the hood, Bobby opens his arms wide, as if in an embrace.

Brad and Nina walk slowly along a sharply curving street past houses set close together on frozen, gray-brown lawns. "Cousin Bobby's clearly a man who knows his own heart," Brad says after a while.

"Pathetic," Nina hisses. She stops the carriage and leans in to look at the baby, who's already asleep. An angora hat with two small, peaked mouse ears covers the baby's head. "Am I prejudiced, or would anyone in the world agree this is one spectacular three-month-old?"

"Oh, I'm sure," says Brad.

"Of what?"

"Wait," he says. "Watch out," and he lifts the carriage over a large patch of swollen concrete, then sets it down gently.

"You're so funny," Nina says. "What a father you'd make."

He assumes she is being ironic, and feels insulted. "You're always doubting me, hinting that I'm incompetent. Even now, when you have no stake at all in anything I do."

"Sweetie pie," Nina says, and grabs his arm urgently. "That

was a compliment back there. I was very moved, thinking what a devoted father you'd be. And actually, I've missed you," she says, leaning her head against his coat sleeve. "Though I guess not our life together."

"In another setting I'd be very desirable, is that what you're telling me?"

"I don't know what I'm telling you."

Rushing toward them from the other side of the street, a gray-haired man in a long tweed coat yells, "Do I see a baby?" He takes a large, awkward step over the curb and looks into the carriage.

"So what do you think, Dr. Glassman?" Nina explains to Brad that Dr. Glassman was her childhood dentist. "One year I had seventeen cavities and spent a whole summer in his office, clenching my fists and staring at the plaid curtains he had up over the window," she says.

"That's not seventeen teeth we're talking about, just seventeen surfaces," Dr. Glassman says. "Now tell me about your wonderful baby. Am I looking at a boy or a girl?"

"Her name is Amanda," Nina says, and pauses. "This is Seymour."

Dr. Glassman shakes Brad's hand. "I congratulate you on your lovely little family, Seymour. And my professional advice is that you enjoy to the fullest these years as a young family. It all passes like a dream; in the blink of an eye it's gone."

Brad nods. He feels Nina's hand slipping into his own. He is light-headed, thinking of his secret life as a husband and father. Soon his child will be grown and he and Nina will be middle-aged, comforting each other in the silence of their empty house.

"Seymour," Nina is saying.

"I'm right here."

"Don't you think we ought to be heading home?"

"Home?"

"Let me just suggest that you wipe the baby's gums with a wet washcloth at least once a day," Dr. Glassman says. "Even at this age." With his back turned to them, he raises a hand high over his head and waves good-bye.

"I'm feeling very lonely all of a sudden," Brad says, and sighs, watching Dr. Glassman disappear into a white Cadillac parked not too far up the street.

"What's the matter?"

"It's the empty-nest syndrome, striking a little early."

"You must think I'm a Looney Tune," Nina mumbles, "trying to pass you off as my husband."

"Don't you know you're talking to a man who drove ninety miles to a party he'd been dreading all week?" And then he is imagining, with astonishing ease, the two of them as lovers, their affair stretching effortlessly over a lifetime, accommodating her marriage, his marriage, children, grandchildren—every obstacle thrown (or carefully placed) in their path. As he envisions it, they won't ever be free to marry each other; really a very romantic notion, he thinks—just what is needed to keep things passionate. Not that he would want to be married to Nina again; he wouldn't dream of altering his life to suit her expectations. But at this moment, looking at her small, round winter-pale face, her eyes large and grave as a child's, he sees that what he has missed most these past two years is the thrill of desire. It seems incredible now that he's managed so long without it, indifferent to nearly everything except his work: women, friendship, the food he prepares for himself, the music he listens to as he falls asleep at night.

"Ninety miles," he says, and puts a hand over hers on the velvety roof of the carriage. He rubs his palm back and forth across her knuckles, no farther. Toward the end of his trip today, crossing the Throgs Neck Bridge, he'd been in such a panic that he missed the outstretched hand of the toll collector entirely, his quarters and dimes falling to the ground and rolling in all directions over concrete. The toll collector, a black woman about his age, looked on with amusement as he jumped from the car and on his knees gathered the coins together breathlessly, as if his life depended upon it. "You one desperate son of a bitch," the woman said, taking the money from him with both hands. Her hair was in dozens of little braids, decorated with beads and leather and thin gold coins. She shook her head at him, and the braids made a tinkling sound, like wind chimes. It was only later, when he arrived at the house and got out of the car, that he noticed his knuckles were bleeding slightly, the skin scraped in layers so delicate they were almost imperceptible.

Drinking champagne punch from clear plastic cups, Brad and Nina sit close to each other on a couch in her parents' den, their knees touching. On the other side of the room people are crowded around an aluminum folding table filled with platters of food. The room is uncomfortably warm. Too many people, too many chairs wherever you walk, too many hanging plants blocking your view out the jalousie windows.

A little girl, about four or so, wearing a long flowered skirt and white patent-leather clogs, is crouched on the step that leads into the den. She stares at Nina. "Where's your baby?" she says. She puts a cocktail frankfurter into her mouth and chews on it a long time. "My mother told me I could play with her."

"The baby's asleep in a bassinet in one of the bedrooms," Nina says. "And you know, the last time I saw you, Janey, you were a baby yourself."

"You have milk in your bosoms?" the little girl says.

Nina and Brad think this is very funny (they look at each other and smile), but Gloria, Janey's mother, who comes along at just the right moment, does not; she yanks her up from the step and says, "Watch your mouth, Lady Jane." Then she taps Brad on the knee, saying, "Terrific to see you."

"If you have any influence at all with your brother," Brad says, "maybe you could get me a whirlwind tour of the neighborhood in his new car."

"Oh, sure." Gloria rolls her eyes. "You came to just the right person."

"What happened to his girlfriend?" says Nina. "Or can't you tell us?"

"She traded him in for a better model, so to speak." Gloria looks startled, as if she can't believe what she's just heard. "Can I talk to you for a minute?" she asks Nina. She pulls at Nina's hand. "It's absolutely imperative."

As Nina rises from the couch and turns so that she is facing him, Brad sees what it is that has unnerved Gloria: two wet stains are spreading across the front of Nina's shiny, off-white blouse. She is leaking milk, he realizes, and then, unexpectedly, he is overwhelmed by a longing to shelter her, to shield her from the husband who speaks to her in a voice that has nothing to do with love.

"I have an announcement to make," Nina's grandmother hollers from the middle of the dining room. "The bride and groom will now cut the cake. I'd like everyone at the table right now. And that includes all those men who locked themselves away to watch football on TV."

Nina has disappeared. From all directions people begin moving toward the dining room table, which has been cleared of everything except a white sheet cake decorated with pink roses set in green-gray leaves, and stacks of dessert plates and silverware. Brad finds himself almost directly behind Nina's mother and father, to whom he hasn't said a word all afternoon. The candles are lit and blown out, then Nina's father is asked to make a speech. What does he have to say after thirty-five years of marriage, Nina's grandmother wants to know.

"Ah, well," Leon says, and clears his throat theatrically. "Life has its little disappointments." A few people, mostly men, laugh uneasily. Then there is silence. "A joke," Leon says, raising both arms in the air. "A *joke!*"

"You'll hear from me later, you stinker," Nina's mother says, but of course she is teasing him, her voice light and friendly as she guides cake into his open mouth with an ornate silver fork.

Leon has just spotted Brad and is motioning to him to come closer to the table. "Hey, buddy," he says. "Are you friend or foe?"

"Happy anniversary," Brad says. Nina's father seems slightly drunk. His smile is goofy, his face flushed and shiny. Brad doesn't like the feel of Leon's hand clamped on his wrist.

"Happy anniversary," says Leon. "And many more."

Nina's mother passes a plate of cake to Brad. "I'm going to cry," she whispers, tipping her head so that it's nearly resting on Brad's shoulder. "If anyone want to know where I am, just tell them I'll be hiding in the bathroom for the remainder of the party."

Leon sighs as he lets go of Brad's arm. "Can I ask you a personal question? Yes? Did I invite you to this party? And if so, why?"

"It was Nina."

"Nina," Leon says, snapping his fingers in front of his face. "Who else." He blinks at Brad. "She's not a happy person, buddy. I don't know how she got that way, and I don't know what to do about it. I spend a lot of time thinking about it, though." His eyes are closed now. "Do you think I'm wasting my time?" When he doesn't get a response, Leon says, "At least there's a baby this time. That's something, I suppose."

Brad says, "I don't think you want to talk to me now. I think what you want to do is slice up the cake and pass it around to your guests, don't you?"

"The thing is," Leon says, "I don't think of it as a waste. There's no such thing as wasting your time when it comes to your children." Accepting the wedge-shaped knife Brad offers him, Leon runs his finger over the serrated edge. "When she was a little girl," he says, "Nina always had to have a rose."

Brad reaches for the knife and skims it along one side of the cake, collecting a row of perfect pink roses. Slowly, with a second knife, he transfers them to a plate that Leon holds solemnly in his hands.

Walking along the narrow hallway that leads to the bedrooms, his fingers curved around the thin china, Brad can feel his hands shaking slightly. Amazed, he stares at his strange coppery fingers, stained, he realizes now, the color of Nina's hair. He presses the rim of the plate into his middle, hugs it delicately, his elbows stiff at his sides.

He finds Nina in her parents' room, nursing Amanda in a blond bentwood rocker. Late-afternoon sunlight falls in narrow bands across Nina's thighs. The baby is asleep; Nina raises a finger to her lips in warning to Brad. She smiles at him, at the roses, but says nothing. The smile has not yet left her face as Brad settles on the floor with his back against the edge of the rocker. In his mind, they are a still life: a mother nursing her child in a sunlit room, while at her feet a man waits patiently, motionless, with a plate of bright roses.

# Aftermath

*A few hours after my mother* died, a friend of hers named Molly showed up in our living room and quickly turned her head left and right, taking in the plastic-covered furniture, the dustless parquet floors, the Wedgwood and Waterford carefully arranged inside the breakfront. "I'll say one thing for your mother," Molly announced to my brother and me, "she certainly kept a nice clean house."

I looked at my brother, whose eyes were drowsy with grief, and hoped that he would tell her to go home, but Stephen only stared at the floor and slumped farther into his seat on the couch.

"No one knows the right thing to say at a time like this," whispered his wife, Annie.

"How do you know?" I said. "Why do you always have to give everyone the benefit of the doubt? You're just like my mother," I said, annoyed at them both, but mostly my mother for her unfaltering goodness.

I was almost twenty-five, and I still believed that my mother had loved me more than anyone ever would. Now there was only my father, who was what my grandmother called "peculiar"—a man who could get angry over anything and harbored grudges almost tenderly, every so often disowning another person from his life until there was only a handful of relatives left he was still speaking to. He knew nothing about the benefit of the doubt.

But most of the family came to the funeral anyway, for they must have known that my mother had shrugged off my father's foolishness as best she could, that it wasn't in character for her to get involved in the arguments that divided the family so predictably year after year.

At the cemetery, my father threw the first shovelful of earth on the coffin, and then flung the shovel wildly into the air.

"He's gone berserk," said my grandmother, wiping first one eye and then the other with the inside of her wrist.

"A maniac," said my grandfather, "but who can blame him?"

When we got back to the house, Stephen told me to wash my hands.

"What for?" I said.

"It's a custom. It could be bad luck if you don't."

"What kind of bad luck?"

"How should I know?"

"I'll take my chances," I said, and hid my hands in the pockets of my skirt.

For seven days we were officially in mourning. At night we had visitors, and my father sat in a velvet chair in the living room in his cardigan sweater and bow tie, but during the day he wore a thin V-neck undershirt and open-backed slippers. Because it was a custom not to shave, his face darkened with unfamiliar stubble, and he began to look like a dangerous man who might have done something unspeakable. He hardly paid any attention to me, or to Stephen and Annie, though he accepted the food we put in front of him, hunching over a bowl of tomato soup or a plate of macaroni. The three of us guarded him in the kitchen as he ate. Stephen, recently out of business school, sat at the table skimming old copies of *Fortune* he'd brought along in his attaché case, while Annie, who was going to be having a baby soon, distracted me with dreamy tales of pregnancy and childbirth, her voice never rising much above a whisper.

When the week was over, I would go back to my apartment in Boston. My last afternoon, I showed my father how to use the washing machine and the dishwasher and stacked a pile of Hungry-Man TV dinners on the shelf in the freezer. My father had never put together even a tuna fish sandwich for himself: all along my mother had sheltered him from the endless work that went into keeping him comfortable.

"Will you be able to manage all right?" I asked, as if it were a matter of carrying heavy suitcases up a flight of stairs.

"I'll survive," he said. He leaned over to kiss me, but I moved when I should have stayed still, and our noses bumped.


Through all the years of my childhood my father and I lived at a distance in the same house. It was my mother who asked all the questions and gathered together all the answers. At bedtime, though, it was my father who got me to sleep. Until I was old enough to do without it, the two of us would put on earmuffs, our makeshift headsets, and stretch out on top of my bed in the darkness until my father, his voice deliberately deep and sober, would say, "Ready?"

"Roger," I would answer.

"Ten-four, over and out," he would say, springing from the bed all in one motion.

This is the only conversation I can remember us having.


In the spring, three months after my mother's funeral, I fly to New York to visit my father. When I get to the house, there's a pile of laundry on the couch in the living room, and when I look in the bathroom, the sink is speckled with turquoise crusts of toothpaste. The soap in the dish is thin as a wafer. Every cabinet door in the kitchen is wide open. Inside the refrigerator, bottles of soda left uncapped have gone flat, forgotten tomatoes and oranges have turned soft and wrinkled. I wonder, as I join my father, who is reading *The New York Times* with his heels up on the coffee table, if other men have done better.

"I think you're going to have to start paying attention to a lot of things," I say.

"I *am* paying attention," he says, and rubs his eyes.

I settle down beside him on the couch, watching as he takes off his wedding ring and examines the circle of pale skin that remains on his finger like a scar.

The next morning, my grandparents arrive with a large carton wrapped in Christmas paper.

"This is a present for you, Nat," says my grandmother cheerlessly, while my grandfather hands the package to my father.

My father tears the wrapping paper and bends over the box. "What am I supposed to do with this?" he says, holding up a bottle of salad dressing.

"It was on sale," says my grandmother.

Soon the kitchen table is covered with jars of mushrooms and olives, tiny cans of chocolate pudding, plastic bags of nuts.

"We know how you hate to shop for groceries, Nat," my grandfather explains.

My grandmother turns to my father. "How can you breathe with all the dust in here?" Her voice trembles. "A grown man, you don't even know enough to live in a clean house."


My father begins to call me every Sunday, though he doesn't like to use the phone, and always speaks into it a little nervously, as if he doesn't quite know what's expected of him. To keep the monthly bills down, he sets the kitchen timer before each call, and when the bell goes off we finish quickly. He talks mostly about the problems he has been having with the backed-up sink, the unreliable toaster oven, the vacuum cleaner that blows dust into the air. It is an endless list of household calamities.

"Why do you let these things upset you like this?" I ask him, after listening to one of his stories.

"I know," he says. "Even Molly thinks I'm overreacting."

"What does Molly have to do with anything?"

"She's been very good to me," he murmurs, and in the background I hear the metallic ring of the timer. "She drives out here after work and cooks some very nice dinners for the two of us. She even makes onion soup from scratch, the kind you get in a French restaurant, the kind with . ."

"I know what you're talking about."

"No you don't," says my father, and he hangs up.

I can see Molly, bony-thin and well dressed, stirring her soup over my mother's stove, maybe even wearing my mother's apron around her waist. She was the only friend of my mother's who'd never been married. As a child I always looked forward to seeing her because of the gifts she brought back for me from her trips: a black velvet sombrero with silver stitching she'd gotten in Acapulco, a handmade Norwegian ski sweater, and my favorite, a handbag from Haiti in the shape of a little thatched-roof cottage. When I was older, I began to notice how she'd sometimes have one drink after another and get very emotional, talking about how much she loved her three purebred cats, and insisting that they were more loving than any three children could possibly be. After her Persian died, when my mother and father had to drive over to her apartment late at night to calm her down, it turned out she was keeping it in her freezer, wrapped in aluminum foil.

Dressed in a three-piece white suit and white Hush Puppies, my father is married to Molly by the same rabbi who had been at the funeral five months earlier. During the ceremony in our living room I watch my father, searching his face for signs of happiness, but to me he looks only stiff and nervous. It is Molly who looks as she should, as if she is in the middle of enjoying the best thing that has ever happened to her. Her head rests against my father's shoulder like a young girl's, openly seeking all the things he's just finished promising her. The moment he slides the ring past her knuckle, I imagine her curled around him on my mother's side of the double bed, and begin to cry.

"Don't do this to me," my father hisses when the ceremony is over.

"What am I doing?" I ask.

"Just be like your mother," he says, and twirls the yellow rose in his lapel. "Be generous."

"I want you and Molly to be happy."

"Well, that's a relief," says my father. "Here I was thinking you wanted us to be miserable."

"Why would I want you to be miserable?"

"You never know," he says.

They travel to the Canadian Rockies for their honeymoon and when they get back my father calls me, sounding tired. "I never see you anymore," he complains. "When am I going to see you?"

"What are you talking about? You just saw me at the wedding."

"That was a month ago. It's the end of the summer already. Why don't I send you the money to fly down and you can spend the weekend here."

"It's only been three weeks. And I thought newlyweds were supposed to be left alone for a while."

"What's so great about being left alone?" says my father. "Why can't I be with my family if I want to? I'm going to call your brother and ask him to come too."

"Molly doesn't want to entertain a houseful of people."

"What people? I'm talking about my children."

"Don't you understand anything?"

There is a pause, and then my father says, "I'll call you back in fifteen minutes."

The next night, when he calls back, he says, "Molly and I had a fight. That's why I didn't call you. But everything's all worked out now. Molly said she'd love to have you come anytime you want."

"She did not."

"Yes she did."

"Tell me her exact words."

"Who remembers exact words?"

"Tell me."

"Okay," he says, and lowers his voice. "What she said was, 'This is your children's house too and I'm perfectly aware that they have every right to be here anytime they please.'"

"Why are you whispering?"

"Molly's asleep," says my father.

"I am not," says Molly, who has picked up the extension. "And your father's a goddamn liar. I said I'd be delighted to see you and your brother whenever you felt like visiting. So we can expect you Friday?"

"I don't think so. David and I are going to be busy painting my apartment this weekend."

"There's no such thing as being too busy to see your family," says Molly. "I want you to come. Bring your boyfriend. Bring his parents too. What do I care? We'll be one big happy family." By now she is crying.

That's when I hang up.

The phone rings in my apartment after midnight. It is a collect call from my father. "What did you hang up for?" he says. "I didn't mean for anyone to hang up." His voice is drowned out by the sound of motorcycles revving up somewhere close by.

"Where are you?" I ask.

"I drove into town. I'm calling from a phone booth outside Burger King."

"Why?"

"Why? Because I can't speak freely in my own house, that's why."

"You haven't even been married a month, and look where you are."

"Why are you blaming *me?*" says my father. "Don't you know all this is par for the course?"

Our silence is filled by a new fleet of motorcycles pulling into the parking lot. "Go home," I tell my father finally. "I'm sure Molly's worrying about you."

"I will. But first I'm going inside and getting a Whooper."

"Whopper," I say, laughing, but then I think of my father sitting for the first time in his life at a plastic table in Burger King, struggling with an unwanted hamburger so big it bewilders him. "Go home," I tell him again.

I get to New York in the late afternoon. Even though I'm the only one coming for the weekend, Molly has filled up apothecary jars with M&M's and jelly beans, as if she were expecting a carload of children to drop by any minute. "What can I get you to drink?" she says, standing over me nervously, gripping the long necklace she is wearing and wrapping it twice around her wrist. "There's Coke, Perrier, coffee, tea, beer, hard stuff."

"You're not running a restaurant," says my father. "Deborah knows where the refrigerator is. If she wants something she'll go into the kitchen and take it."

"Let me be a good hostess in my own house, if you don't mind."

"What do you mean, hostess? What kind of a word is that to—"

"No one's asked me how my plane ride was," I interrupt. "Actually, one of the passengers forced the pilot at gunpoint to take us to Newark. That's why we came in a few minutes late."

"Are you sure you don't want something to drink?" says Molly.

"Maybe later."

"Did anyone ever tell you you're very hard to please?"

I stand the jar of jelly beans in my lap and take out a handful. "How did you know how much I like these?" I say, and put them in my mouth two at a time.

"It's too late for that now," says Molly. Then she runs for the front door, the beads around her neck clicking angrily. My father doesn't go after her.

"I should go back to Boston," I say.

My father shakes his head. "She's very touchy these days. You look at her the wrong way and you're in trouble. I don't think marriage is the best thing in the world for her."

"It can't be easy, after living alone for so many years."

"Being alone, being together, none of it's easy," says my father.

Outside it darkens and suddenly begins to rain, and soon Molly is back, silently wringing the water from her hair onto the floor in the foyer. My father and I stare at the outline of her underwear showing through her rain-soaked dress. "Stop looking at me," she yells. Later, when she comes down to make dinner, she is wearing a bright green kimono and so much perfume that my father has to open three windows. She seems to have forgotten her anger, humming "You Are the Sunshine of My Life" while she sets out chopsticks and soup bowls filled with rice on the dining room table. I stand at the doorway of the kitchen watching her cook our dinner in a stainless-steel wok, and then I carry it to the table for her. My father looks into the wok and makes a face.

"What's wrong?" says Molly.

"We always have chicken on Friday night," says my father.

"That's what's on your plate right now: Triple Fragrance Chicken."

"I'm talking about *roast* chicken. It's a tradition in this house. We used to have it every Friday."

"Well, I'm starting a new tradition."

"Promise me you'll make my chicken for me next Friday."

"I resent the fact that you would even ask something like that of me."

"What did I ask for that's so terrible?" says my father. He grabs my hand from the table. "Deborah?"

"I'm keeping quiet," I say.

"You just tell your father he better watch his step," says Molly. "I'm not one of those relatives he doesn't have to speak to if he doesn't want to. I'm his wife. He has to deal with me for the rest of his life."

My father talks quickly. "I only have enough change for the first three minutes," he says. "Can you believe Molly accused me of spending too much time on the phone with you?" It is the third time this week he has called.

"She's right," I say, unable to admit how moved I am by this compulsion of his to tell me nearly everything that happens to him.

"If I wanted to talk to you ten times a day, that's my business."

"She's your wife. Everything you do is her business."

"Today she wanted to know who meant more to me, you or her. I told her it was a stupid question and I wasn't going to answer it. She was furious. She knocked all my clothing in the closet onto the floor. Then she finished off half a bottle of gin, got into her Mazda, and left." Suddenly it sounds as if something is caught deep in his throat.

"What is it?" I ask. "What's the matter?"

"Signal when through," says the operator.

"Where are you?"

My father clears his throat and breathes hard into the phone. "At La Guardia," he answers. "I decided to take a little trip and come and see you. I thought we could hang around Harvard Square together or maybe rent a car and drive out to Provincetown."

"I have to go to work tomorrow."

"No you don't. Just call them and say your father's unexpectedly grown old and sick and incapable of taking care of himself."

"Would you stop it! I couldn't even meet you at the airport," I say. "You'd have to take a taxi."

He arrives in the middle of the eleven o'clock news, dressed in a raincoat that is missing two buttons and carrying a Sabena Airlines bag over his shoulder. Although I've lived in the apartment for nearly a year and a half, this is the first time he's ever seen it. "Do you have any ginger ale for me?" he says as he takes off his raincoat.

"How about something else?"

"Never mind." He points to the little sleeping loft above us. "What if you wake up on the wrong side of the bed and fall down the stairs?"

"Don't worry about it."

"The steps are too close to the bed—it's not safe. I don't like the idea of you living this way," he says.

"You're tired," I say. The strip of silvery blond hair that is always combed across his bald spot is out of place, hanging awkwardly below his collar. I lean forward in my chair and flip the hair back to where it belongs.

"Don't do that," he says sharply, his hands flying to his head. "Only your mother could do that."

Without speaking, we go our separate ways and put on our pajamas. Up in the loft we settle into twin beds, pushed a foot apart.

"Good night," I say to my father, thinking it is more than he is entitled to.

"Ten-four," he murmurs.

# Light-years

*I*n the kitchen, on the refrigerator door, held there by a magnet disguised as a tomato slice, is a snapshot of a pair of tiny blond children. The picture was taken outdoors, at dusk, and you can barely make out the faces of the boy and girl, who are dressed in the simplest of Halloween costumes: they are two white-sheeted ghosts, dangling hollow plastic pumpkins from their wrists. Sometimes when Mark looks at the picture, he imagines that the children are related, a brother and sister separated by just three months. The little girl, Dana, is his daughter; the boy, Patrick, is his upstairs neighbor's son. The picture was taken eight months ago, shortly before Mark and Nancy, Patrick's mother, became lovers. Lovers. The word pains him, because it reminds him that he has betrayed his wife for the worst reason—no good reason at all. (In his mind, anyway, boredom and restlessness are pretty poor excuses. Only love is an acceptable excuse, and what he and Nancy are up to probably hasn't much to do with love.) His wife, Laura, whom he married six years ago, is a vice-president of a bank in the city; she commutes into Manhattan early every morning and returns home long after Dana has gone to sleep for the night. Mark is a free-lance writer. He has a contract with a publisher to complete a book on the pleasures and perils of self-employment. He started work on the manuscript two years ago, when Dana was born. He wrote while she slept, which in those days was for hours at a stretch. Now she only naps for an hour in the early afternoon, time he usually spends in Nancy's bed.

The book, if it ever gets finished, is not something he will be proud of. The project has gone sour for him, like milk abandoned in a far corner of the refrigerator, lost in a clutter of newer, fresher things. He will never admit this to his wife, who is a hotshot young executive, a woman who loves her work. And whenever he tries to confide his fears to Nancy, he sees her face go blank—he can almost hear her mind shutting off with an audible click. This is puzzling to him, because sometimes their friendship seems as satisfying as any of those he had in high school and college long ago. The number of hours the two of them are together each day amazes him; that they haven't had a serious argument or grown tired of each other's company amazes him even more.

They are like two young mothers who meet every day at the same park bench, with so much to say that they are constantly interrupting each other, astonished, and grateful, for all that they seem to have in common.


"Fries and ketchup," Dana says in her small sweet voice. "Restaurant." She is sitting on the living room floor, paging slowly through a department store catalog. She is naked except for a rainbow-striped canvas visor and a necklace of plastic walnuts, almonds, and cashews. Her clothes are in a pile next to her.

"You planning on going to the restaurant naked?" Mark says. "You want strangers to laugh at you?"

"Okay," Dana says, without looking up from the catalog.

"No clothes, no restaurant. It's as simple as that," Mark says. For weeks now, Dana has been stripping numerous times throughout the day, whenever the mood strikes her. When he told Laura about it, she laughed with real pleasure, as if she had been listening to a funny story involving imaginary people. She had missed the point entirely—that he was sick of spending so much energy struggling to get Dana into her clothes. His wife is living on another planet, light-years away; a place that seems to grow more distant from moment to moment.

"Fries and ketchup," Dana says again. "A lot of ketchup."

"A deal's a deal," Mark says, picking up her Miss Piggy T-shirt and trying to squeeze it over her head. Dana grabs the shirt and throws it to the floor. "I see," Mark says. "That's fine. We'll have lunch at home." From the refrigerator he chooses a package of English muffins and a jar of grape jelly. He toasts a muffin and sets it out on a plate for Dana, who is standing in front of the television set switching the channel selector like a madwoman.

"Luncheon is served," Mark says. "And incidentally, if you break the TV, you'll have only yourself to blame."

Dana climbs onto a chair in the small dining area outside the kitchen and examines the plate. "Egg McMuffin," she says.

"That *is* an Egg McMuffin," Mark says.

"Egg please."

"We don't have any eggs."

"Why?"

"Let's just say I've been remiss." Mark lowers his head, rubs at the space between his eyebrows.

"Daddy making me crazy."

"What?" He looks up at her, startled. He watches as she takes small quick bites from the muffin and stores them in her cheeks, which immediately grow puffy. "Swallow," he says. "Don't eat like that." He wonders, not for the first time, if he's really not a very good father at all, but the kind Dana's analyst will be hearing about in detail twenty years from now. He thinks he's a decent parent—patient and accommodating and affectionate—but maybe he's already made a thousand irreparable mistakes. He and Nancy talk about this often, exchanging worries about their kids' terrible habits: Patrick's refusal to drink anything but Hawaiian Punch, Dana's willful vomiting whenever she doesn't want to go to bed at night. His life, contrary to all expectation, is by no means simple, Mark thinks, watching carefully as Dana starts to swallow her food. His wife misunderstands; she thinks raising a child is, like most other things, merely a matter of common sense. Recently she complained to Mark that he looked worn-out, that he had a pallor, that his posture was like an old man's. What's your problem, she wanted to know. Any idiot can take care of a child. Then her face reddened. That's not what I meant, she said. I just keep thinking you're making it more difficult than it has to be. She changed the subject, asked how his manuscript was coming along. Not bad, he told her. She smiled, looked relieved. Good for you, she said with a little too much enthusiasm. Things are going so well for her, exactly as planned. He'd like her to feel a little guilty for that, but he sees no sign that she does. He's the one with the guilt, a lump in his throat that will not go away. Two different doctors have told him the lump is psychosomatic; not an uncommon thing, they both said in the same soft voice. As if that would make him feel better.

"Can you give your dad a pat on the back?" he **asks** Dana. She shows him her hands, which are dark with jelly. He cleans them with a washcloth and hitches her up on his hip. She pats his back lightly several times.

"More?" she says. She pats him again, harder.

"Thanks very much," Mark says. He is aware of a slight noise at the door, then hears the knob rattling. Suddenly the door swings open and Patrick rushes into the living room, followed by Nancy. She's dressed in a peacock-blue jump suit that reaches a little past her knees and beige sandals with high heels. She has two gold earrings in each ear, a crescent of moon and a star. This is the first he's seen of her today, though normally, in good weather, they're out on the lawn behind their apartments before nine o'clock. "So what did Patrick think of school?" he asks her.

Nancy laughs and flops down on a maroon velveteen love seat. "All the mothers left their kids in the basement of the church and then took turns staring through the peepholes that were drilled into the walls. You could see your kid live, in living color, having a perfectly miserable time. Or the time of his life, as the case may be. Anyway, I've been advised to try again in six months or so."

"Peepholes?" Mark says.

"You never heard of peepholes for spying on your kids?"

"Never." He smiles at her. She's an extremely pretty girl in her early twenties, with dark eyes and long light hair in a permanent that's half grown out. At seventeen she left home and moved in with her boyfriend, who became her husband a few years later. Before Patrick was born, Nancy worked in a dentist's office, where she dressed in a lab coat and answered the phone and sent out the bills. She gave up her job willingly, though recently she's been talking about going to college and then dental school. She spends her free time reading Gothic romances by authors with false-sounding names, and has crazy taste in movies—*The Exorcist* is at the top of her list—but it's easy for Mark to ignore these few failings. He's never had a female friend before, or known anyone like her; anyone who bypassed college and headed straight for love.

He has told his wife that they are friends, and a few facts about Nancy's life. Laura couldn't imagine his having anything much to say to someone so unlike himself, but she was glad he'd found a friend over the age of two to keep him company, she said. At least she understood that much.

"Got any big plans for the rest of the day?" Nancy asks him. She goes to the refrigerator, looks around for a while, and settles on a handful of green olives from a small jar.

"Grapes," Dana says, stretching out her hand for some.

"Olives," Nancy says. "Believe me when I tell you they're

out of your league entirely." Opening the refrigerator again, she takes out a bottle of club soda.

Dana stands up on her chair. "Soda for Dana, please."

"Jesus Christ Almighty!" Nancy says good-naturedly. "May I or may I not finish my lunch in peace?"

Mark tells her she can give Dana some soda in a juice glass. His eyes are on Patrick, who has gone into the kitchen and is pressing a row of buttons at the top of the dishwasher. A red light glows; the machine begins to hum. Nancy slaps her son's hand; he laughs at her and slaps his other hand, saying "No no no."

Nancy turns the machine off. "I thought we could take a drive out to the beach this afternoon. Maybe these two will give us a break and fall asleep in the car."

"Dana's got to have a haircut. Orders from my immediate superior," he says, rolling his eyes. "Anyway, it's true that her bangs are hiding half her face."

"I'll do it," Nancy says. "What do you want to pay someone ten dollars for when I can do it for free?"

"There's that place in the mall," Mark says. "I promised I'd take her there."

"Promised who?"

"I thought you like the mall."

"We spend half our lives there," Nancy says. She writes some numbers in the air with her index finger, then a multiplication sign, a horizontal line, and more numbers. "More than half," she says. "More like three-quarters."

"You can't argue with numbers," Mark says.

Nancy sighs. "Lend me a diaper and I'll be ready to leave in a minute."

"Help me dress her and I'll buy you a balloon at the mall."

"I couldn't possibly accept a balloon from a married man," Nancy says. She grabs Dana by the waist, kisses the top of her head, and carries her off to the floor. Mark works quickly; by the time he's finished, there's a mustache of perspiration above his lip.

Just as they are about to leave, the phone rings. It's Laura, who says she has a free minute and wants to chat. "What's new at the zoo?" she says. She lowers her voice. "I miss you," she says. "How do you like that?"

"It's lonely at the top, I'm sure."

There is a pause, and then his wife says coolly, "May I talk to my child, please?"

"I was teasing you, honey," he says. "Joking."

"Is Dana there or not? Where is she?"

He hands the phone to Dana. "Talk to your mother," he tells her. "Say something heartwarming."

"Know what?" Dana says into the receiver. "Know what?" She hangs up the phone.

"Very unwise," Mark says, waving a finger at Dana. "You used extremely poor judgment, honey."

Nancy says, "You'd better call her back."

"Let's keep the line free and see what happens." Nothing happens; then he dials his wife's number and gets a busy signal. He waits a few minutes and dials again.

"No luck?" Nancy says.

"It's probably a business call."

"I'm sure she's trying to get you."

Mark shakes his head. "Into the car, all of you."

Nancy gets Patrick's car seat and sets him up in the back next to Dana. Up front beside Mark, she flips down the sun visor with the mirror attached to it and puts on plum-colored lipstick. Her arm settles over the back of the seat, behind Mark's shoulders. If they were in love, he thinks, her hand would find its way to his shoulder blades, to the warm skin under his collar. But neither of them ever touches the other, except in bed. He is very conscious of this, of the limits of their connection. But it's just as well: his head is still above water, and he does not intend to go under.


At the mall, the four of them troop over to Shear Magic, where the hairdressers wear clown suits, and instead of barber's chairs, you have your choice of a fire engine, a sports car, or a taxicab. But the place is closed when they get there. SEE YOU NEXT MONTH WHEN WE OPEN UNDER NEW IMPROVED MANAGEMENT a sign in the window says.

"Don't worry about a thing," Nancy says. "We'll go home, I'll dress up in my clown suit, get out my scissors, and we'll be all set."

Mark says, "Forget the clown suit. Let's simplify, reduce life to its lowest common denominator and all that."

Nancy looks at him. "I like that," she says. "Did you just make that up?"

"Me?" He makes an effort not to smile. "I'm flattered," he says. "Really."

"Don't tell me," Nancy says, holding her arm out in front of her. She closes her eyes. "Philosophy 105."

"American Literature to 1830," he mumbles, embarrassed. "But philosophy was a good guess."

"You think I'll make it through dental school?" Nancy asks him. "Or do you think it's all fantasy? Tell me."

He tries to picture her in a lab coat, studying X-rays, earnestly lecturing a patient on the proper way to floss. But he can only see her as she is now, absently stroking her son's hair with her fingertips, as he's seen her do so often.

"You're so young," he says. "There's plenty of time for things to happen."

"Sure," she says. "Of course." Her voice is almost a whisper. "I keep telling myself that this is my life for now, that later it will just be something I've lived through, like high school or a boring summer when I was a child . . ."

He nods his head, envying her plans, all the years she has coming to her that he's already used up. He thinks of a time when, for him, everything about her will be indistinct, vague and shadowy as a half-remembered dream.

"What?" he says. Dana is dancing between his knees, pointing to the frozen yogurt stand where they sometimes stop for a cone. "All right," he says. "But first I'd like a pat on the back for a job generally well done." He swings her up from the ground and savors her palm against his back, a touch so gentle his eyes burn with sudden tears.


Nancy's apartment is exactly like Mark's—a small two-bedroom with a front door that opens directly onto the living room, which, like his own, is taken up by a couch and a matching love seat and a square glass-topped coffee table. "Sorry for the mess," she says as he follows her into the kitchen, where everything is immaculate, and in perfect order.

"Don't be crazy," Mark says. "Why do you always say that?"

"Do I?"

"I'm not your husband," he says. "I don't have a dirt detector that buzzes every time some microscopic bit of dust crosses my path."

Nancy turns on the faucet and washes the few dishes that are sitting in the sink. "He's not that terrible," she says. "It's mostly me, just trying to keep one step ahead." She dries her hands on a pale green paper towel. "You want to find fault with him," she says. "You're dying to hear me say I have a bad marriage, as if that would somehow make everything valid. Or at least half valid." She grabs at his sleeve with her damp hand, leaving a small dark stain on his shirt. "It wouldn't give me any satisfaction at all to hear you bad-mouth your wife. I don't even know her—knowing that she's a terrible cook or a bad mother means nothing to me."

"She's not," Mark says. "Who ever told you that?"

"My husband," Nancy says, "is really a very nice guy."

He nods his head. Her husband is red-haired and muscular, and, as far as he can tell, very amiable. Whenever Mark happens to run into him—usually at the vast container at the back of the parking area where they dump their garbage—her husband smiles a serene and patient smile at him. He comments on the weather and asks about Dana, and then, because they are neighbors who barely know each other, there is nothing left to say. Just seeing him for a minute or two at the garbage dump is enough to make Mark sweat through his shirt. The lump in his throat swells until it seems to fill his chest and he can hardly breathe. Like a criminal who sends anonymous letters to the police, he has an overwhelming urge to confess. He fantasizes about the note, crudely spelled out in letters cut from newspapers and magazines, that he will slip under his neighbor's door in the middle of the night. *Someone you know is in bed with your wife weekdays at noon.*

"Listen," Nancy is saying, "it's really not such a serious business."

"What?"

"Falling in love with someone. Or not falling in love. Either way, you survive."

He stares at her, wondering if she could possibly be in love with him, then decides he'd rather not know. He prefers to let things remain as they are, unexamined and undisturbed, like the tiny splinter of wood that has been sitting for months just under the surface at the bend of his wrist. He prefers to concentrate on their favorite subject, their children, the one subject that can seal any silence between them.

"Where are those two?" he says, and suddenly the radio is on at full volume and he sees, in the living room, Patrick and Dana dancing with surprising grace to a Rod Stewart song. He rushes into the room and turns down the volume. "You crazy teenagers don't know a thing about respecting the rights of others," he says, smiling at them, but they've already lost interest in the music and are heading in different directions, Dana toward the telephone that hangs on the wall just outside the kitchen, and Patrick into his bedroom.

"I'm ready to proceed as planned," Nancy says, coming at Dana with a comb and a pair of scissors in one hand and a plastic spray bottle filled with water in the other. She's wearing mouse ears from Disneyland on her head; the name "Gregory" is spelled out in orange thread at the back of the hat.

Dana drags a chair to the phone, climbs up on it, and lifts

the receiver. "Mommy. Office. Work. Job. Thank you," she says rapidly. She hangs up the phone and sits down.

"I assume that was a business call." Nancy holds up the plastic bottle and says, "Do you know what I'm going to do with this?" She turns around and aims the nozzle at Mark, spraying his hair so that water drips down the sides of his face and into his ears. "See," she tells Dana, "there's nothing to it. First I zap your father and now I'm going to zap you."

"Who's Gregory?" Mark says, wiping the water from his face with his fingers.

"Gregory was my beloved golden retriever," Nancy says. "He died of cancer just before Patrick was born. I don't want to talk about it." She busies herself with Dana, wetting her hair down, then combing through it slowly and carefully. "It's a shame," she says. "Her hair is thin and very fine, a fatal combination." She looks at Dana with pity, and then at Mark.

Unexpectedly, he is very depressed: his daughter, for whom he's wished perfection, has lousy hair. He touches the flawless skin of her cheek in consolation.

"No," Dana says. She pushes his hand away and slides off the chair. "No."

"I still have dreams about him now and then," Nancy says. "I wake up in the morning and that's who I'm thinking about. I wanted to name Patrick after him, but my husband thought it was too bizarre, naming a child after a dog. He said, 'Picture this kid going through life knowing he's been named in memory of a goddamn dog.' I told him it was better than being named for your father's lover. It's true," Nancy says, mocking the surprise on his face by opening her mouth wide as his own. "My mother never knew until years later, when I was about seventeen. She thought my father just happened to like the name Nancy for no particular reason at all."

"Christ," Mark says. "Jesus." The story has given him a headache, a pain that beats dully across his left eyebrow.

Nancy says, "You better believe it. My mother went wild when the truth finally came out. She made my father sleep on the floor next to their bed for a couple of weeks. He tried to convince her to let him sleep on the couch in the den, but she wouldn't let him out of her sight. She wanted to change my name to Priscilla, which was what she'd wanted to call me in the first place. She offered me a new car in exchange for changing my name. Too bad: it would have been nice to have had my own set of wheels."

"Poor lady."

Nancy shoots him a look; he understands that in her eyes, his sympathy is misplaced. "People do such strange things to their kids," she says. "You think I've ever forgiven my father?"

He thinks of Dana, and of Patrick, witnesses recording everything they've seen and heard. He sees himself, middle-aged and awkward, sitting down with Dana in a darkened room, putting all the pieces together for her, trying to make some sense of the facts.

"I'm going to take Dana home," he says. "We can try the haircut some other time. Tomorrow," he says, seeing how disappointed Nancy looks.

"Stay," Nancy says. "Just stay until five o'clock. At five I start believing the day's going to come to an end; I can start thinking about dinner, about the sun eventually going down . . . You know what I'm saying."

"Yes," he says. He leans forward, and with his arms at his sides, kisses her, surprising them both.


After the seven o'clock news, when he is giving Dana her bath, Laura calls again. He carries the bedroom phone into the bathroom and sits with it in his lap. He keeps his eye on Dana, who is drinking grayish bathwater from a small plastic canoe. "Delicious," he says.

"What?" Laura says.

"When are you coming home?"

"You really piss me off," Laura says.

"Your daughter, you may be interested to hear, is guzzling bathwater even as we speak."

"Here I am working my head off—"

"In your ivory tower high above Wall Street, secretary at your beck and call, anticipating your every need."

"Be serious," Laura says. "You're a real joker."

"Untrue. Most of the time I'm as disheartened as the next guy."

"What's the matter?" Laura says. "I count on you to tell me things, but you never do."

Through the vent in the bathroom wall he hears Nancy singing in a high-pitched voice to Patrick, "Merrily merrily merrily merrily." Often, after they've parted for the day, he listens to her talking to Patrick, laughing with him, and late at night, humming to herself as, he imagines, she brushes her hair, touches perfume to her collarbone before joining her husband in bed. He feels as if he's spying on her, without risk, taking in lovely bits and pieces of her that she unknowingly gives away.

"It's not as if I'm not interested," Laura is saying. "That's not it at all."

Nancy's voice sails throught the vent like a breeze. "At night the stars put on a show for free / Darling, you can share it all with me-ee."

"What can I do for you?" Laura asks. "What?"

"Dana wants to talk to you," Mark says.

"Did she get a haircut today?"

"It didn't work out."

"What does that mean?"

"You don't have a good grasp of how these things work," Mark says. "Nothing is as simple as you think it is."

"We're talking about a haircut. I can say with all certainty that I have a pretty good grasp of the material," Laura says sarcastically.

"Goddamnit." Dana is squatting above the water, peeing, a washcloth draped along her shoulders like a cape. "I can't talk to you," Mark yells, and hangs up the phone. "You're driving me to an early grave," he warns Dana as he lifts her out of the tub. "You and your mother are some pair."

"Mommy," Dana says with enthusiasm.

Once Dana is asleep, he takes a joint from a hollowed-out book that says *An American Treasury of Humor* on its spine. He smokes it at a leisurely pace, then sprays the living room with air freshener, because who can tell what kind of mood his wife will be in when she gets home. His clothes are spicy with the scent of dope, but he's too lazy to change them. And breathing in the familiar odor, he begins to smile. He ought to do this more often, he thinks, just sit quietly by himself and let his mind go blank for a little while every day. Soon his stomach is rumbling and he realizes he should be thinking about getting dinner together. It occurs to him that he's had no lunch, just some yogurt he shared with Nancy at the mall. Nancy. He remembers the way she looked today, lounging cheerfully on the love seat in her bright blue jump suit, searching through his refrigerator, bending to kiss the top of his daughter's head. In bed the other afternoon, she'd whispered possibilities he has not allowed himself to think about: the possibility of a new job for her husband in Atlanta; the possibility of a loss that she and Mark would have to bear on their own. He is in a panic now; his heart races, his eyes cloud with tears. Without her, he will be a man getting up in the morning without hope or desire. He will go through the motions; change diapers, love his daughter, wait for his wife to come home so they can both collapse on the couch with the newspaper and the TV and not much else.

He hears Laura fumbling with her keys at the door. She steps inside, stands her attaché case and a small shopping bag against the wall. "Hi-honey-I'm-home," she says, running the words together, their private joke in imitation of all the TV husbands they grew up with.

"Dinner," he says, getting up from the couch and slowly coming toward her.

"What about it?" She takes off her suit jacket and steps out of her shoes, drapes the jacket over a side of the playpen that stands at the back of the dining area.

"What are you in the mood for?" he asks her. He hangs the jacket in the closet.

"No thoughts on the subject whatsoever."

"Are you angry at me?"

"No," Laura says. "Should I be?"

"There's salad in the refrigerator. Why don't I go out and get a pizza?"

"I went to an Italian restaurant for lunch today," Laura says apologetically. "Business lunch." She describes the meal: melon and prosciutto, tortellini salad, strawberries with zabaglione for dessert.

"Sounds nice. Lucky you," he says.

"I ate too much," Laura says. She puts her arms around his neck, kisses him on the mouth. "Destroying your brain with illegal substances again?" she says lightly.

"Guilty." He shrugs his shoulders.

"What time did Dana get to sleep tonight?"

"About an hour ago," he tells her.

"Was that before or after you lit up?"

"How would you like a punch?" he says, folding his fingers into a fist and shaking it at her.

"I was teasing, of course."

"Well, I denies the allegation and I resents the alliga-tor."

"You're all confused," Laura says, smiling at him. "Let me show you what I got for Dana today." From the shopping bag she takes a red-and-white toy television set with Disney characters printed on paper behind the plastic screen. She turns a knob and the characters float across the screen; a music box plays "It's a Small World." "Pretty nifty," she says. "What do you think?"

He stares at the toy, which Dana had got as a gift from a friend last winter. He wants to remind Laura what she has forgotten; to lead her by the wrist to Dana's toy chest, to humiliate her, to make much of her ignorance, of how little she knows. Will you look! he wants to shout at her, his hand held firmly at the back of her neck.

Watching Laura studying the television set as intently as a child, he remembers falling effortlessly in love with her, remembers a time, not long ago, it seems, when she could do no wrong. He nods his head now, smiles in her direction, saying, "Pretty nifty."

Later, lying in bed with Laura motionless beside him, he listens, or imagines he is listening, to the soft muffled sounds of Nancy and her husband making love just overhead.

He has slept only two hours when Dana wanders through the dark into their bedroom and announces it is morning. She wants Cheerios and orange juice, she says, trying hard to push his head from his pillow.

"Take it up with your mother," he says. "Tell her exactly what you want." To Laura he says, "Take a guess at what time it is." When he gets no response he says, "Just a wild guess."

"Is this a dream?" Laura says. Her voice, coming from under the blanket she's pulled over her head, sounds as if it's very far away. "Is this the Twilight Zone?"

"Wait a minute and I'll check." His hand skims his daughter's face. "Are you for real?" he says. "Because if you are, you're in big trouble."

"Trouble," Dana says, laughing. She says it twice more; clearly she likes the sound of the word.

"Would you please go back to bed," Mark says. "You don't want your mother and father to have unhappy memories of your early years, do you?"

"Do you want to come and sleep with us, baby doll?" Laura asks. "There's room for you right here," she says, patting a small space on the bed between the two of them. "The best seat in the house."

"No," Dana says.

Mark says, "Can't you find a soft spot in your heart for those who love you best?"

"Cheerios."

Clenching his teeth, he starts to get up, but Laura stops him with a hand on his elbow. "I can handle it," she says. She rolls over him and out of bed. She is a small straight figure standing at his side in the dark. "You've covered for me a thousand times." Picking up Dana, she moves toward the door.

"It isn't that," Mark calls after her. "It's not a matter of that at all."

Alone in bed, he rests his head on his arm and listens carefully for the small sounds of activity in the dining room; the sound of Dana's spoon knocking sharply against the plastic cereal bowl, the sound of Laura yawning into her hand as the sky slowly lightens beyond their windows.

He will not sleep any more this morning; knowing this, he walks barefoot through the apartment until he sees Dana asleep at the table, a spoon in each hand. Laura is on her knees on the couch, looking over the top of the cushions at the sunrise.

"Pretty," he says, and falls into a corner of the couch next to her.

She stares straight ahead, her body perfectly still.

Mark says, "Maybe, if we're lucky, we can get her back into the crib without waking her."

"It's so funny, really," Laura says in a faint voice.

"Funny?"

"That morning, just before she was born, that last hour or so before it was all over, I thought, if I live through this, I can live through anything; that nothing else would ever be this hard." She looks at him, her face puffy with weariness. "I want to know what you were thinking," she says. Her voice grows stronger. "I want to know."

What he remembers is the moment of birth; the surprising violence, and a vividness of color—Laura's bright blood everywhere, the baby blue-gray, looking like something unearthly. And he remembers himself clearest of all, so choked with fear it was as if he and Laura had been in mortal danger.

Gathering Laura's hair, fine as a baby's, behind her shoulders, he weighs it delicately in his hands with his eyes closed. She is holding her breath, waiting for an answer. He lets go, lets her hair fall without a sound against her shoulders.

"I can't remember," he says.

# Markings

*That morning when her marriage* unofficially broke up, and her husband, Michael, moved into a friend's brownstone apartment all the way over on the West Side, Ellen tried for hours to get her mother on the phone. By the time she got through to her, the fingertip she had used for dialing was swollen and circled by a black ring. "You should have had the operator cut in on the line and say it was an emergency," said her mother, after she heard that Michael had left with several cartons of his favorite books, and not just a suitcase full of clothes.

The breakup had been Michael's idea. They had been married for five years (five comfortable, easy years, Ellen thought), and then one winter night, just as they were about to undress and go to bed, Michael said that their life together had turned out to be a disappointment for him. He sounded apologetic and admitted that he was probably one of those people who would never be satisfied with anything for long. There were sharp pains in Ellen's stomach as she listened to Michael talk and watched him crack the joints of his fingers one by one. She kept her hands pressed against her middle, though it did no good at all. Without warning, their cat,

Benjamin, an orange tabby who had been with them since the beginning of their marriage, jumped into her lap and covered the white star on his muzzle coyly with his tail. "Not now," said Ellen, and dropped him to the floor. When the pain had traveled upward to her chest, she said to Michael, "I think I have a terrible case of heartburn. Or indigestion."

"Let me see what we have in the medicine cabinet," said Michael, and came back with a bottle of Pepto-Bismol. He poured some into a spoon for her and after she swallowed it she began to cry. Michael sat down next to her on the bed and picked up her hands and rubbed them, as if she had just come in from the cold. "I have to do what I do," he said as Ellen pushed his hands away. "I can't let my life go on being a disappointment to me. It wouldn't be fair."

Ellen said, "Get away from me, you jackass," when Michael tried to help her undress, and then she got into bed in her underwear. All that night she stayed awake, trying to figure out what she would do. A dozen times she saw herself getting dressed and going to work, then drew a blank. For a long while she stared at Michael, at the long bones of his limbs bent peculiarly in sleep, and then, very carefully, she drew his arm around the curve of her shoulders. Still sleeping, he nestled against her, spreading warmth along her spine.

In the morning, on the subway headed for her office, she cried discreetly, her head bowed, her fingers stretched open across her face in a fan.


Michael found himself a girlfriend right away: a painter, a daring girl with four earrings in each earlobe and frizzed-out, ginger-colored hair. She lived in a studio apartment in the East Village and slept in a bed in a corner of her kitchen, to give herself more room to paint. Ellen had gone with Michael once to a party in her apartment and immediately had decided that Pamela was someone she could admire—an artist with talent, a tall, graceful, interesting-looking girl who dressed in costumes and got away with it. When Ellen heard that Michael and Pamela were lovers, she understood. She could imagine him caring tenderly for Pamela, soaping up her shoulders for her in the shower, kissing her under a hard spray of water, writing their names together in a heart on the bathroom mirror misted over with a ghostly steam.

It was after she found out about Pamela that Ellen first noticed the small white spot on the underside of her wrist. Later she found similar markings on her back and in between the bumps of bone below her neck. It seemed to her that the smooth white patches were growing larger, and finally she went to the doctor, who had to look it up in a textbook. "I'm pretty sure it's something called vitiligo," he said as he put the book back on the shelf. "A loss of pigment. It's probably nerves, that's all. Maybe you need some help working out the things that are bothering you."

"I'm fine," said Ellen. "I'm not a nervous person. I'm very low-keyed."

"Suit yourself," said the doctor, who was young, and wore expensive leather running shoes. After looking around a minute for his prescription pad, he wrote down the name of a psychiatrist on a piece of paper which was stamped DUMB THINGS I GOTTA REMEMBER NOT TO FORGET. She crumpled the paper into an ashtray on her way out of the office.

On a Friday evening, six weeks after Michael's leaving, Ellen is eating a circus car of animal crackers for dinner, and looking out the row of windows in her living room as she eats. The apartment is near the East River and on the ground floor of the building. According to the super, every tenant who ever lived on the first floor put bars up over the windows as soon as he moved in. But Ellen and Michael could never bring themselves to do it, and then, one Sunday afternoon, just at the moment they walked into the apartment, someone tossed a hammer through the bedroom window. Michael yelled at

Ellen to get away from the glass, saying that he would take care of everything. He was a natural at taking care of things—cooking dinner night after night, keeping track of the bills, sewing patches on Ellen's dungarees for her, remembering to collect quarters so they could do the laundry.

Outside, it is mild and summerlike, though it is only the start of the first weekend in April. Benjamin is asleep on the windowsill. Through the open window Ellen watches as an elderly man wearing earmuffs makes his way down the street. A woman with a sleeping baby strapped to her back in a canvas carrier comes up rapidly from behind. She smiles and says that spring is here as she passes the old man.

"What?" The old man lifts the earmuffs away from his head.

"I was just saying that spring is certainly here now."

The old man squints, and shakes his head.

"I said spring is here, goddamnit," says the woman, and crosses over to the other side of the street, swinging her arms angrily.

Ellen is still feeling sorry for the old man when a kid about sixteen carrying a big black transistor radio comes by and urinates on the small rectangle of grass beneath her window. Ellen raps on the glass as the kid tucks his shirt in his pants. He looks up at her and grins. "Everything's cool," he says. Then he turns up the volume on his radio and dances briefly to some disco music, his eyes closed.

Ellen draws the drapes over the windows and lies across the couch on her stomach with a copy of *Other Men's Daughters*, a favorite novel she is reading for the third time. It is an intelligent book about adultery. She understands that the world is filled with adulterers, with people on the make. She and Michael were peacefully married for five years and she never suspected that for a long time Michael had been fantasizing about being on the make.

She had fallen in love with him when they were both in high school. He was the first boy in their school to grow his hair below his collar and wear wire-rimmed glasses. Ten years later he liked to take out the yearbook and show people how cool he looked, even in 1968, when everyone else looked like an insurance salesman. Ten years later his hair was still longer than everyone else's. Whenever Ellen's father saw him he annoyed Michael by saying, "Didn't anyone tell you that long hair is out?" The last time Michael bought any new clothing was in 1968. Nineteen sixty-eight was the best year of his life. He had a girlfriend and a '67 Triumph, a TR-4A that never gave him a minute's worth of trouble. He totaled the Triumph in a supermarket parking lot right around the time he and Ellen were married.

She had been six weeks' pregnant then, though that had nothing to do with their getting married. Ten days after the wedding she had an abortion. When she came out of the sodium pentothal, everything was whirling and she had cramps in her stomach. The people at the clinic gave her some hot coffee, but it only made her vomit. All during the ride back to the apartment in a taxi she moaned and dug her fingers into Michael's wrist. Later in the day, when she was feeling well enough to sit up in bed and eat some noodle soup, Michael said that he had been convinced she was going to die and that right there in the taxi he had begun rehearsing in his mind what he would tell her mother and father. Ellen thought that was hilarious and was surprised at the troubled look that appeared on Michael's face as soon as she started to laugh. When he told her he didn't think she ought to be so irreverent, she said, "Listen, the only thing I can't be irreverent about is our marriage. If you ever wanted to divorce me I'd kill you." Then it was Michael who started to laugh. He talked about how his grandparents had gotten divorced forty years ago. It was all because his grandfather refused to get a job and spent his time sitting in front of the house eating cherries and spitting the pits into the street.

The only other time either one of them mentioned divorce, Ellen remembers, was the day Michael had to go to court about a traffic ticket. He had gotten the ticket for making an illegal left turn in her father's car on a deserted street in Nassau County, but it happened only because the sign forbidding it had been turned around by the wind and couldn't be seen. Michael went to court with a carefully prepared diagram drawn on oak tag with different-colored Magic Markers. The diagram showed exactly the way the sign had been facing. The judge sitting in that day smiled at Michael and said, "I hope to God you're not planning to go to law school. You'd be a real pain in the rear end, you know that?" Michael had to pay the fine anyway, and on the way out of the courthouse he kicked a water fountain so hard that he cracked a bone in one of his toes. The toe turned purple, then in a few days green, then yellow. Some doctor in an emergency room charged forty dollars to read the X-rays and wrap a Band-Aid around the toe. Ellen told Michael that if he ever showed his temper like that again their marriage would be over.

The phone rings. Ellen thinks about the possibility that it will be Michael, calling to report that living without her is making him miserable. Ellen has been waiting to hear this since the morning he left her. What she would do eventually, she thinks, is forgive him his selfishness and help him move his clothing and books back into the apartment.

It turns out to be her mother, Connie, calling from the phone booth on the corner, asking if Ellen would like to go out for dinner.

"I've already eaten," says Ellen, who wants only to stay home and read about adultery all night.

"All we had in mind was a light supper."

"I just finished off a whole box of animal crackers. I'm stuffed. Really."

Connie sighs into the phone. Then she says, "Daddy will feel terrible if you don't come out with us. He's waiting at the front of the building with the car."

"You always do this to me, damn it," says Ellen. "You're so good at making me feel as if I don't have any choice."

"Good," says Connie. "I'll meet you outside in a few minutes."

Ellen puts on a pair of gray pants and an expensive black blouse that Michael gave her for her birthday. Over the years he bought all her presents with care; blouses and jewelry and books that she was happy to have. Her mother used to say Michael was a gem, one in a million. Lately she's been saying he's a mixed-up kid who doesn't know whether he's coming or going. Ellen doesn't know what her mother would say if she knew about Pamela.

As Ellen gets into the car, Connie swivels around in the front seat and says, "It's a pleasure having a daughter who lets you come to see her without calling her first for permission. I know parents who have specific instructions never to drop by unexpectedly. Imagine how awful it must be to be afraid to visit your own children."

"It's the psychiatrists who are responsible for that nonsense," says Ellen's father, Hal. "You go to one and the first thing he tells you is that your parents are at the root of all your problems. And you know, in certain circles the analyst's word is the word of God. If an analyst told these people to jump off the top of the Empire State Building, they'd do it."

"Well," says Ellen carefully, "it would have been nice if you'd warned me you were coming."

Hal weaves their car swiftly in and out of three lanes of traffic, cutting off several drivers in his way. Connie braces herself against the dashboard and says, "Could you try to drive like a decent human being, please?"

It is true that Hal drives like a madman, speeding whenever he can and slamming on the brakes at the last possible moment. It has always been this way. Hal is an otherwise careful, patient man. When they stop at a red light he looks at Ellen in the rearview mirror. "What do you hear from Michael these days?"

Ellen shrugs. "I have his phone number, but I'm only supposed to use it in an emergency."

"My heart hurts me when I hear something like that," says Connie. "Fortunately, you almost never hear things like that in our family."

"You really don't," says Hal. "There was, in fact, only one divorce that I'm aware of. And that includes both sides of the family."

"What happened?" Ellen leans forward, folding her arms along the top of the seat behind her mother's head.

"It was a long time ago. One night, in the middle of the winter, one of my cousins told his wife he was going out to get some oranges. P.S. he hopped on a plane to Florida and never came back. He did send his wife a bag of fruit, though."

"I don't believe it," says Ellen. "There must be more to the story than that."

"I'm telling you the facts as I know them," says Hal.


The restaurant, which serves forty different kinds of crepes, is almost empty of customers. The waitresses look bored, leaning against the wall with their arms crossed behind them, occasionally smoking cigarettes and whispering in French.

As they linger over a shared cup of chocolate mousse, Ellen's parents try to persuade her to come home to Long Island with them for the rest of the weekend. "It's important for you at a time like this to be with the people who love you," says her mother.

Ellen rolls her eyes and says, "What are you so worried about? I'll be all right. I went to the library yesterday. I've got plenty of books to read."

"Too much solitude isn't good for anyone," says Connie. "Haven't you noticed that all the psychopaths you read about in the paper are always described as loners? They eat one meal after another by themselves, in a little corner somewhere, and then one day something sets them off."

Ellen smiles. "I'm not going to go berserk," she says. "All I want to do is go home to my apartment."

"That's okay with me," says Hal. "Just let me take care of the check." A waitress comes to the table immediately, without being called. "*Pendant la deuxième guerre mondiale, j'étais en*

*Paris,*" says Hal casually, as he reaches for his wallet. He memorized the sentence more than thirty years ago, when he got out of the Army, and it has always given him pleasure to try it out on people. The waitress, who is old enough to remember the war in great detail, nods her head slightly, just enough to let Hal know she heard him. "You can pay the cashier up front," she says, and walks back to her station against the wall. The table is silent; Hal's ears, small and delicate-looking, have in an instant turned scarlet.

"To tell you the truth," says Connie finally, "except for Maurice Chevalier, I've never thought the French were a particularly nice people."

Hal pays the check and the three of them walk back to the car. Connie and Hal hold hands; Ellen walks behind them. Many years ago, when she graduated from high school and they took her to Paris for two weeks in the middle of the summer, the three of them had walked along the Seine exactly as they are walking now. Hal had asked Ellen to stay behind them, saying that a walk along the Seine was meant for lovers, and that someday she'd have her turn. She kept her distance from them that afternoon, taking small, slow steps and all the time thinking of Michael, wondering how she would ever manage to see him again since they would both be living away from home at different schools in the fall.

As they speed down Second Avenue in the Buick, Hal whistles "Someone to Watch Over Me," then, "But Not for Me," dragging out each note poignantly. All Ellen can think of is poor Gershwin dying of a brain tumor in California. "You're giving me a headache," she tells her father. "Don't you have anything cheerful in your repertoire?"

"Let me think about it," says Hal.

Soon there are signs for the Queens Midtown Tunnel, signs with arrows pointing toward Long Island. "I can't believe you would do this to me," says Ellen as she reads the signs. "I can't believe you would sink so low!"

Her mother tells her father that Ellen is not a child anymore. "The time when you could force her to do the right thing is long gone," she says, making it sound like a lament.

"Benjamin has to be fed," Ellen hollers, growing more distracted as they approach the entrance to the tunnel. "If you're going to kidnap me, will you at least let me make sure there's enough food in his bowl to last the weekend?"

"Cats can go without food for forty-eight hours," says Hal. Now he is whistling "I'll Be Down to Get You in a Taxi, Honey," slapping his hands on the steering wheel every few beats.

"When you were a little girl," says Connie, "you promised that when you grew up you would buy the house next door to ours and move in there with your husband. You thought that would be the greatest thing in the world."

"You had no right to do this to me," says Ellen. "I'm talking to both of you."

"I know that things are different now," says Connie. "I know the big thing is moving to California and getting as far away from your family as you can."

"Sure," says Ellen. "I bet I could be very comfortable three thousand miles away from you, seeing you once or twice a year, getting a letter every now and then."

Her mother makes a noise that sounds like the squeak of a small animal. Then she begins to cry.

"Why are you doing this to me?" says Ellen. Now it is clearly she who must make amends. She bends over the front seat and kisses the side of her mother's neck. The skin is warm and smells faintly of Shalimar, which comes out of a tiny bottle she opens on special occasions. Ellen cannot remember the last time she saw her mother's tears.

Connie hunches into her corner of the car. "You've always taken good care of me," says Ellen. She slides her hand over the slope of her mother's skull. Over and over, until her mother finally says, in a voice so tiny it is nearly inaudible, "Forgiven."

Hal is doing seventy-five on the expressway. "You know,

I really love driving this car," he says, turning to look first at Connie, then Ellen. "I get behind the wheel and I'm in seventh heaven."

Saturday night, Ellen and her mother and father sit down at the dining room table to look at family pictures. Her father has dozens of boxes of slides that document her life. They show that Ellen has hardly changed at all since childhood, that she has always looked vaguely foreign, her face full-cheeked and sallow, her eyes and hair nearly black.

"As you got older, you became an increasingly less cooperative subject," says Hal as he flashes a slide on the dining room wall. Everyone laughs: there she is on her thirteenth birthday slouched grimly against a blossoming pear tree in the front yard. Pinned to her chest is a corsage made of bubble gum.

"Apparently that was during my awkward stage," says Ellen.

"You never had an awkward stage," says her mother. "You were always a delight."

They come to a box of more recent pictures. The first one in the batch shows Michael standing behind Ellen with his arms crossed protectively around her waist. His hair is in a thin blond ponytail and there is a gentle, sleepy-eyed expression on his face.

"What a sweetheart he was," says Connie. "I never thought a boy like that would go and do something so stupid."

Hal shuts off the projector and switches on the lights. "Listen," he says, "before I go to sleep tonight I want to know if my daughter and her husband are ever going to live together under the same roof again. I want to discuss things."

"Would you mind leaving me alone, please," says Ellen. She rubs at a small white blotch in the crook of her arm.

"What am I, a stranger who doesn't have the right to ask about your personal life?"

"Can't you ever give me a break?" Ellen gets up out of her

chair and rushes past the kitchen and out the side door, a route she has taken in anger many times. She sits down on the curb near the front lawn, her elbows resting on her knees. She has forgotten how dark and soundless it is away from the city, how sweetly peaceful. If she were still a smoker she would certainly be having a cigarette right now, she thinks. According to Michael, who figured it out on a calculator, she had smoked seventy thousand cigarettes before quitting, had shortened her life expectancy by almost six hundred days.

She is sitting on the curb where Michael used to park his Triumph the summer before they were married. Every week-end night that summer they sat in the car and talked. Often they stayed there talking until the sun came up and the people in the neighborhood came out in their bathrobes to walk their dogs. From the car they could see Ellen's mother periodically peeping through the blinds in the bedroom. At daylight, when they came inside for something to eat, there would be two places set at the kitchen table for them, and a blackout cake in the refrigerator, and sometimes the carcass of a turkey or chicken breasts left over from dinner. They ate silently, exhausted, and when they were finished, Ellen always walked Michael to the front door and waited there with her eyes half closed until he shifted the Triumph into first and disappeared around the corner, gears scraping against the early-morning stillness.

She tries to remember exactly what they talked about for all those hours. Mostly books and writers, she thinks. "The Death of Ivan Illych," which they decided was the greatest story anyone had ever written. *Nightwood,* which neither of them could finish. Whether Virginia Woolf would be remembered as greater than William Faulkner. How Sinclair Lewis could possibly have won the Nobel Prize.

After a while they began to talk about marriage, though they never mentioned the word itself and could only say, "If we end up together," pretending in the phrase which sounded so casual that things could go one way or another, that it was simply a matter of waiting to see what would happen. During their last year in college, when they had finally become lovers, Michael told her about the day he had bought his Triumph in 1968 and how he had driven over to her house hoping she would be impressed with his car and go out with him. But no one had been home, and so he had gone to see someone else instead—his second choice, but a girl who might go out with him nevertheless.

Ellen was not surprised to hear this and she accepted it as proof that fate had been keeping them apart until just the right moment—that chilly summer morning when they bumped into each other on the Long Island Railroad and looked one another over carefully for the first time in three years.

Once they were married, Ellen kept hearing from her friends that the first year was all uphill. She didn't know what they were talking about: she and Michael were getting along as well as they always had. He was in graduate school studying American cultural history then, and she had just started working as a reader for a small literary agency near the Forty-second Street Library. Every night when she came home from work Michael had dinner on the table, tricky things like chicken parmigiana, lasagna, and Chinese dishes that he cooked in a wok. The only thing she and Michael ever had serious arguments about was all the cigarettes she smoked, and when she gave it up, he joked around and said that now she was absolutely perfect, that he couldn't think of a single thing to complain about.

And it was always difficult for Ellen to complain about *him:* she never confided a long list of grievances to any of her friends. At her desk at the literary agency she sat and listened, day after day, to women complaining about men, to an over-flow of accusations and reproaches that were willingly shared with anyone who happened to be at the nearest desk. The stories told illustrated what everyone listening already knew —that men were experts in inflicting pain, and ultimately, and one by one, would show themselves to be unworthy of love.

Hearing the stories, Ellen, so far from the center of things, wondered how she had managed to live such a charmed life.

She stares now at the hazy night sky, suspecting that tomorrow it will rain and she will be stuck all day in the house where her parents' disappointment lingers everywhere in corners, like dust.

Sunday, Ellen wanders barefoot into the kitchen, wearing one of her father's undershirts for a nightgown.

"What would you like for breakfast?" says Connie. She looks soft and chubby in her bathrobe, which is floor-length and made of turquoise velour. The skin under her eyes is shiny with Vaseline—the only thing that will really ward off wrinkles, she thinks.

"What time is it?" says Ellen, watching the rain that slaps against the kitchen windows.

"Eleven thirty. It's been raining like this all morning."

"You shouldn't have let me sleep so late." Ellen rummages around in the cabinets over the sink, and brings a box of Hydrox cookies over to the table.

"Why can't you eat like a normal person and not aggravate me?" says Connie. She opens the door to the refrigerator and takes out a large Lucite tray of hard-boiled eggs, tomatoes, and three different kinds of cheese. In the center of the platter is a cup of water filled with carrot sticks.

"What's all that food for?" says Ellen. She dips a Hydrox cookie into a glass of milk and waits for it to get soggy.

"I want you to have some of this," says Connie. "I know you're not eating properly. How much do you weigh?"

"Ninety-one," says Ellen, trying to put the whole cookie into her mouth at once. Half of it breaks off and sinks to the bottom of the glass.

"Ninety-one." Her mother shakes her head. "What am I going to do with you?"

"How about giving up?"

"*I* don't give up on the people I love."

Ellen sighs, and stretches her arms out over the table, crossing her wrists in front of her. She studies a new white stain just above her elbow. Then, suddenly, she starts to laugh, remembering what she was dreaming about just before she got up this morning. In the dream, she awoke in her apartment with a star-shaped smudge of white on her nose. As she examined herself in the mirror, she could see that the white marking was exactly like the one that was spread over Benjamin's muzzle. She decided to draw some whiskers at the corners of her mouth with an eyebrow pencil, and then went off to work, where she got one compliment after another.

"What's so funny?" says her mother, and smiles.

Ellen, still laughing, looks around the small, crowded kitchen. "Did I tell you Michael has a girlfriend who sleeps in a bed in her kitchen?"

"Bastard," her mother says swiftly.

Ellen is embarrassed to be laughing so hard. She doesn't want her mother to think she is crazy. She stands up and starts to back out of the room.

"Where are you going? Stay here." Ellen bites on the inside of her mouth, trying to keep back the laughter. She walks around the table to where Connie is sitting. "Here," says her mother, pulling Ellen down into her lap. Ellen settles herself against the softness of her mother's bathrobe. She tries to sober up fast by thinking of something that will do nothing less than break her heart.

She imagines Michael and Pamela making love in Pamela's kitchen, under the long wooden spice rack that runs above the bed like a headboard. She sees the rack collapsing on them, and Michael and Pamela in a bed littered with oregano and parsley. This strikes her as very funny: she continues to laugh. Her stomach aches and her eyes are filled with tears from the strain of laughing so hard.

"Talk to me," her mother begs.

# Skaters

*H*enry's son and granddaughter were there to meet him when his plane landed at Kennedy, on New Year's Day. The first thing he noticed was that Robert and Rebecca were unusually pale, as if they hadn't quite recovered from the flu. Looking around, he was relieved to see that they were no paler than anyone else; then he saw the down coats and fur jackets and remembered he was no longer in Florida.

A few weeks before Thanksgiving, his son's wife had left him for a woman she'd met at a health spa. It was a Jack La Lanne, ten minutes from home, in Manhasset, and she'd met the woman in the spa's tiny indoor swimming pool. When Robert had told him all about it over the phone, Henry couldn't think of anything to say but how awful he thought the whole thing was; he hadn't offered to come up North, even though he sensed that was what Robert wanted from him. Retired and a widower, he enjoyed a life that was peaceful and well ordered; he just didn't want to be drawn into the heart of someone else's disaster. And he suspected that in living alone he had lost his gift for being patient with people, that he no longer knew how to be of comfort to anyone.

He was a big, solid-looking man, with thick silver hair, and he had spent more than half his life as a guidance counselor in a junior high school in Queens. He had savored the work, mixing easily with students and parents, thinking of himself as a psychiatrist, social worker, and counselor all in one. Every day at three forty-five, when he left school, he had closed his mind to whatever had happened at work and gone straight home to help his wife, Sally, fix dinner. He liked to spend the last hours of the day in the little bathroom he had turned into a darkroom for himself. Summers, when school was out, he and his wife traveled, cross-country and to Europe. In Florida, where he went after he lost Sally, it was always summer, and the days were his to do with as he pleased.

Robert had waited until Christmas to tell Henry the news, and as Robert went on talking Henry began to think about how much he hated New York in the winter. He remembered the windows that leaked icy air into his old bedroom in Forest Hills, the mounds of filthy snow on Queens Boulevard, the freezing wind that made his cheekbones ache. Thirteen hundred miles away, in Fort Lauderdale, he shivered.

"I'm bereft," Robert said into the phone. "Utterly."

After a long silence, Henry said, "Well, I guess I'll call a couple of the airlines and see what I can do about getting up there."

"Thank God," Robert answered.

As they waited now for his luggage to come around on the carousel, Henry buttoned his raincoat against the chill. He watched his son closely, looking for evidence: anything at all that would show that here was a man whose life was a shambles. Robert looked the same as always—like a high-school kid who would probably grow to his full size in a few more years. He was just five-six, blond and slight. What he needed was a full beard and mustache, but every time he stopped shaving he got colorless wisps that appeared to have settled onto his face by accident. For years Robert had confided in Henry, and Henry knew that before his marriage he had been disappointed by one woman after another, most of whom ended things by accusing him of being "too nice" or "too generous." When Henry had called to tell Robert the flight he'd be on —a call that cost Henry thirty-three dollars—Robert admitted that the accusations had always struck him as self-contradictory, and that it wasn't until his wife left him that he understood he'd been mistaken. (Listening to Robert, Henry nodded his head yes, thinking that anyone in the world could have told his son how wrong he'd been.)

"Isn't that your suitcase?" Rebecca pointed to a plaid zippered bag that had a large white H made out of masking tape on the front.

Henry pulled it off the carousel just before it moved out of reach. "Thanks, Miss Eagle Eyes," he said.

"You're welcome. Want to hear me use the word *meretricious* in a sentence?"

"What?"

Rebecca grinned. She was ten, but she looked like a miniature adult. She was wearing dungarees, a navy blue turtleneck sweater, and a dark green down vest. Her ears were pierced and in each one there was a tiny gold hoop. "We wish you a meretricious and a happy new year," she said, and then she giggled.

"Very clever," Henry said. He wasn't exactly sure what *meretricious* meant but thought it had something to do with prostitutes. Last year, before he moved to Florida, he'd learned that Rebecca had been designated a gifted child, and that she had been put into a special class at school. He wondered just how much a child like that could be told about why she'd been abandoned by her mother. No matter how gifted she was, he decided sorrowfully, the information was bound to screw her up.

Henry insisted on going with Robert out to the parking lot to get the Datsun and on carrying his suitcase himself. In the car, Rebecca sat up front with Robert, and Henry in the backseat with his suitcase. "Did you know you're my precious girl?" he said, leaning forward and twisting Rebecca's hair into a braid like the one she'd worn last winter.

"Don't," Rebecca said sharply, and jerked her head away. "You're going to wrinkle my hair. I like it nice and straight."

"Excuse me." Henry could feel his face warming; under his raincoat perspiration dampened his shirt. He unzipped his suitcase and pretended to look for something that was buried at the bottom.

"Anyone have any ideas about dinner?" Robert said.

"I wouldn't mind McDonald's," Rebecca said, "although I have to say their french fries usually aren't as good as they're supposed to be."

"That's fine with me," Henry said. He didn't tell them he'd made a hamburger for himself for lunch.

At McDonald's, Robert settled Rebecca at a table in back while Henry went to give their order. The girl who took the order seemed bewildered when Henry asked for a Big Mac without lettuce and special sauce. "What's the point?" the girl said. "It makes no sense. You might as well just have a regular cheeseburger."

When their order was ready, he looked into the bags and saw that she had given them small Cokes instead of large ones, and that she had forgotten their McDonaldland cookies. For a moment he debated what to say to her, and then very carefully he said, "It doesn't matter, really, but I think I ordered the other size soda and some of those cookies."

"I've been telling myself all day that this job has got to go," the girl said, wiping tears from her eyes.

"It's all right," Henry said. "I just flew in from Florida, and they gave us a nice snack on the plane. So don't worry about it."

"I need this dumb job to stay in pharmacy school. Do you have any idea what that costs me?"

Robert stepped in front of Henry and grabbed the bags from the counter. "Let's get this show on the road," he said.

"Good luck," Henry called over his shoulder as Robert

steered him toward the table where Rebecca was waiting. "That was very rude of you. I'm surprised at you," he told Robert when they sat down. He took his hamburger out of the Styrofoam box and was about to take a bite from it when he noticed a man sitting alone at a table across the aisle. The man had very short hair, pale blond except for a patch of turquoise at the side of his head. There was a studded dog collar around his neck and a safety pin through his earlobe. Henry put down his hamburger.

"No good?" Robert said.

"That man over there—"

"Punk-rocker," Rebecca said. "Don't you have them in Florida?"

"Why would anyone do that to himself? It doesn't make any sense."

*"Chacun à son goût,* if you know what I mean," Robert said. "What else can I tell you?"

After Rebecca went to bed, Robert fixed Henry tea in the kitchen, Henry's favorite room in the house. The kitchen had a slate floor and a large fireplace, and there was an oak icebox and an antique rocking chair Polly had stripped and refinished herself. Swedish ivy hung from the bay window, which had a pretty view of the pond just beyond the backyard. Henry waited nervously for Robert to start talking about Polly. He was always a little uneasy talking with his son, afraid that something he said might be misinterpreted by Robert and hurt him. Robert had never had much of a sense of humor about himself; he was always on guard against insults. Once, when he was about sixteen, and Henry had casually suggested that he was old enough to start going out with girls, Robert had turned on him in a fury. "It's great knowing your own father has doubts about you," Robert had yelled at him. "Thanks a lot." Henry, so successful in dealing with other people's children, instinctively knew the right thing to say to everyone but his son. All he could do was approach Robert with caution, and keep his fingers crossed.

In the kitchen they discussed the Cuban refugees in Miami, and whether or not Henry should trade in his five-year-old gas-guzzler for a Honda or a Rabbit. Soon Robert began to yawn and rub his eyes, and Henry relaxed—obviously Polly wasn't going to be mentioned at all until the next day. But then, looking down into his teacup, Robert said, "I'll never get over this, you know. Not in a hundred years."

Henry was silent.

"I wish I could have fallen out of love with her the moment she told me what was going on. But I'm still waiting."

"Well, it makes sense," Henry said. "You don't just lose all feeling for a person overnight. It has to be more like a leaky faucet, where you lose a little at a time. But anyway, what you have to do is tell yourself that things always work out for the best. And they do."

"I hate it when you talk like that," Robert said. "It sounds so idiotic."

"What do you want? Do you want me to tell you that Polly's as good as they come, and that this is the worst thing that could have happened?" Henry was thinking about his sixtieth birthday last spring and the party Polly had made for him. She had baked him a very professional-looking heart-shaped cake, which, she said, was certainly appropriate under the circumstances. When he asked what she meant, Polly said, "Just that we're all crazy about you, that's all." To Henry she had always seemed sweetly transparent, not like all the people he knew who went out of their way to keep you guessing about their private selves. That was why he had so much trouble believing she had run off with a woman. He had thought homosexuality required a great deal of sophistication—something he had been convinced Polly just didn't have. She had a husband, a child, and a house, and he was sure she had taken pleasure in all three. When he still lived in Forest Hills, he had made it a point to visit every other weekend and he had seen with his own eyes over and over again how well Robert and Polly fitted together, both of them so eager to please each other. Even a stranger could have seen in a minute that they belonged together.

"She'd been sneaking into the city to go to Gay Alliance meetings," Robert said to Henry in a whisper. "She and Amber had this thing going for almost three years." He shook his head. "The two housewives."

"Three years?"

"Keep your voice down. This is a small house."

"I'm sure there are doctors who specialize in this sort of thing," Henry said. He was talking very fast. "They show you your mistakes. Eventually you can be cured." He did not want to believe that the marriage was beyond repair; if he had to choose between Robert and Polly he would not be at all sure of what to do.

Robert rolled his eyes. "You're missing the point," he said. "This is what she wants. This is what makes her happy."

"She was happy with you until she met this Amber."

"Wrong," Robert said. "There were other people before Amber. This goes back a long, long time."

"So why did she marry you?" Henry yelled. "For what possible reason?"

"I just had the bad luck to be in the right place at the right time. And how many times do I have to ask you to keep your voice down?"

"Rebecca," Henry said more softly. "What's going to happen to her?"

"She wet her bed four nights in a row this week," Robert said. Resting his elbows on the table, he fitted his palms together as if in a salaam and pressed his teeth into his fingertips. Henry noticed then that Robert was wearing two watches, one on each wrist. He had to ask why.

"I just got this one a few days ago," Robert told him, pointing to the digital watch on his right arm. "I don't really trust it yet, so I wear my old one, too."

"How will you know when you can trust it?" Henry said.

Robert seemed surprised at the question. "I'll just know," he said.

Henry woke up in the middle of the night. The room was freezing. His first thought was that he had left the air conditioner running, and he got out of bed to turn it off. He walked barefoot to the window and tripped over a barber's chair Polly had got at a garage sale one summer. He realized where he was: thirteen hundred miles from where he wanted to be. After his wife died, when he had made the decision to retire and move to Florida, Robert had tried to talk him out of it, saying it was crazy for him to spend the rest of his life so far from the people who cared about him most. "You just concern yourself with your wife and daughter," Henry had told him. "I'm old enough to watch out for myself." He didn't tell Robert how fearful he was of being drawn to their house too often, and then one day finding he was no longer welcome. And he wasn't someone who believed that children owed their parents anything; whatever he had done for Robert had been done willingly and lovingly, and he had no wish to be repaid. There were friends of his in Fort Lauderdale who couldn't stop weighing and measuring, who always thought they deserved more from their children than what they had got. One of his friends, a woman he used to play backgammon with, had kept a running tab of what it cost her to raise her son. The day of her son's wedding, she told Henry, she showed him the complete bill, "just so he'd know what's what in this world." Henry avoided the woman after that, and, as it turned out, never talked to her again. It wasn't that he considered himself an exemplary father. He had got used to being at a distance from Robert's life, and found that he preferred it that way; preferred not to know that his granddaughter wet her bed, that his son was distrustful of even the watch on his wrist. He did not want to know all the things that he was helpless to change.

Wrapped in an afghan, and wearing the rubber thongs he usually wore to the pool, Henry made his way down the stairs to the kitchen. The teacups and saucers and spoons were sitting in the sink, where Robert had left them. Henry washed and dried them and put them away. Waiting for the sun to come up, he swept the kitchen floor and set the table for breakfast. Even with the afghan he was cold, but he wasn't about to fool around with the fireplace and he couldn't find the thermostat to turn up the heat. Finally, it occurred to him to switch on the oven. In a little while he was warm and drowsy, settled in the rocking chair.

Rebecca was mixing an envelope of Instant Breakfast into a plastic mug when he woke up. She was wearing a blue floor-length nightshirt that said "Yale Sleeping Team" and red furry slippers that showed her toes. She put a hand on her hip and continued stirring her milk. In a comic, high-pitched voice she said, "Instant Breakfast, for your information, is not a meal."

"What?" Henry said.

"My mother said that ten times a week. She used to try to get me to eat all kinds of things with it, but I never wanted to. Now I can do whatever I want, without too much of an argument."

He asked if she saw her mother a lot.

"She takes me roller-skating and ice-skating. Sometimes Amber comes, too. She came yesterday," Rebecca said.

"So what's Amber like?" he said, trying to sound casual.

"I think she's probably the skinniest person in the world. She tried to kill herself once. She jumped out of a window and broke her back. She was a very unhappy person. But now she's with my mother, and they're happy. It's my father who's unhappy. That's why I'm supposed to make an effort not to aggravate him. The doctor I go to tells me that all the time. He's Chinese. Amber always says, 'What's new with Dr. Sun Yatsen?' even though I keep telling her that's not his name."

"I have to have some coffee," Henry said. "Do you want some?"

Rebecca looked at him. "Children don't drink coffee," she said.

"Oh, sure. I was just kidding." While Rebecca was talking, he had poked all ten fingers through openings in the afghan's stitching, and now he saw that he had probably ruined it. He tried to get up out of the rocking chair but collapsed on his knees because both his legs had fallen asleep.

Rebecca ran to him. "Are you all right?"

He was embarrassed. "I'm fine," he said, and stood up.

Rebecca slapped her hand to her chest and panted dramatically. "I was so scared. I thought you were having a heart attack."

"Don't be silly."

"I know. But I thought everyone's grandfather had a heart attack sooner or later. That's just what happens."

"Not in this family."

"Want to hear me use the word *isthmus* in a sentence?" Without waiting for an answer she said, "Isthmus be my lucky day!"

"You bet," Henry said.

Because he was curious to see Polly and Amber, Henry let Rebecca talk him into going to the roller-skating rink with her Saturday. The week had been quiet; Henry had kept busy with housework and gone to afternoon movies to pass the time while Robert was at work and Rebecca in school. Rebecca had plans to meet Polly in front of the snack bar at one o'clock. Robert was making his weekly trip to the supermarket, the cleaner's, and the library, and would pick up Henry and Rebecca on his way home.

"I'm nervous," Henry told Robert in the car. "I know I'm going to say the wrong thing. Like on 'The Odd Couple,' where Felix warns Oscar to be careful not to offend the midget, who's very sensitive about his size. So what do you think Oscar says when they're introduced: 'It's nice to meet you, Mr. Midget.'"

"She's the one who ought to be nervous, not you," Robert said. He dropped Henry and Rebecca off in the parking lot and turned back into traffic.

Henry had never been to a roller-skating rink before, and he wasn't very impressed with what he saw—the rink reminded him of the gymnasium in his old junior high. It was big and drafty and obviously hadn't been cleaned or painted in years. At exactly one o'clock, Polly skated over to them. Amber was just behind her. Polly kissed Rebecca and hugged Henry. Her dark straight hair was like Rebecca's, and her face was round and very pretty, though she was wearing so much makeup Henry wondered what she was hiding. She and Amber were dressed in royal blue satin shorts and little white T-shirts. No one would have guessed that Polly was close to forty. Amber, Henry decided, couldn't have been more than twenty-five. She was as skinny as Rebecca had said, and much taller than Polly. All he could think of was Mutt and Jeff. When Polly introduced Amber to him, Amber shook his hand and said nothing. But she bought Rebecca a frankfurter at the snack bar, which pleased Henry a lot.

"You look nice and tan," Polly told him after she had sent Amber and Rebecca off to skate together. "How's it going at the condominium?"

"The pool had a couple of drowned mice floating around in it a few weeks ago," Henry said, "but we took care of it. Other than that, everything's been going smoothly."

"You're happy there?"

"I have more friends now than I've ever had in my life. And I have my golf and tennis and Spanish lessons and my photography. And if I knew that my family was all in one piece, I'd have no complaints at all."

"Let's go and sit down," Polly said evenly. "We skated for almost an hour before you got here. I'm exhausted."

They seated themselves at the end of a long bench that was in front of a wall of lockers. The rink was crowded, mostly with teenagers, but he was surprised at the number of adults who were serious skaters, showing off solemnly in the center.

Over the PA system, a woman's voice was singing something about hot love or hot stuff—he couldn't quite make out the words. Polly was tapping one skate to the music. "Great song," she said, and he remembered Polly and Robert practicing dancing to "their" song—"Embraceable You," he thought it was—in the living room in Forest Hills, days before their wedding. What had she been hoping for then? That the years with Robert would pass as painlessly as possible until one day she'd be fearless enough to go after what she really wanted? She'd put on a good show all those years—he had to give her credit for that. Of all the people he knew, he would have said that she was among the happiest, the most content with her life. He had never seen her anything but cheerful. Henry's father used to say that only idiots were happy all the time, but his father had been a terrible pessimist. Like Robert, who even as a child had seemed surprised when things went his way. Asking permission to go to the movies, or to stay up an extra hour, or to have a friend sleep over for the night, Robert had hung his head apologetically and looked down at the floor. As hard as Henry tried, he could not warm to a boy like that. "What are you staring at? Are there diamonds on the floor?" he would say, pretending annoyance, when really he was worried sick that this child whom he loved so deeply had so little confidence. Years later, when Polly said she would marry him, Robert wouldn't take yes for an answer, and half a dozen times he'd asked if she was sure. Since their wedding, whenever he had a question or some problem to discuss, Henry found himself turning first to Polly, and in its way that closeness had almost been enough.

"Listen," Polly said to Henry. "Why don't you go rent a pair of skates and we'll go around the rink together a few times."

"No thanks, I gave at the office," Henry said.

Polly laughed. "I promise I won't let you fall. You can hold on to me every step of the way."

She was already half off the bench; he could see that she

couldn't sit still anymore. "Go," he said. "It's all right." When Polly skated off he noticed that her shorts were too small—a little bit of her behind was visible, and he sensed it wasn't accidental. Anything was possible, he saw then. She might kidnap Rebecca and try to keep Robert from seeing her, or she might just as easily disappear with Amber, never to be heard from again. He didn't trust her.

Henry got up off the bench and walked to the low wall that circled the rink. There was a railing around the rink on both sides, and he leaned over and rested his arms against the metal. It took him a while before he spotted Rebecca. The three of them had formed a chain—Polly in front, followed by Rebecca holding on to her mother's waist, and then Amber, her arms around Rebecca's middle. They shrieked when they saw Henry, and Polly waved. They made their way around the rink twice before an attendant in a neon orange uniform caught up with them. The man pointed to a large sign that said eating, drinking, smoking, chains, and other horseplay were forbidden on the rink. Frowning, he grabbed Rebecca's hands from Polly's waist and then took off, skating backward into the crowd. Henry watched as Rebecca, and then Polly, rushed off the rink. He ran to meet them. Rebecca was in tears, her head drooping so that her chin touched her chest.

"She wants to go home," Polly said. "I told her she was being silly, but she won't listen."

"Robert isn't supposed to pick us up until about five or so," Henry said. He paused, listening for Polly's offer to take them home.

Polly knelt beside her daughter on the dirty wooden floor. "You're a big girl," she said with her eyes closed. "You better get your act together. You can't flip out every time someone looks at you cross-eyed."

Rebecca lifted her head. "We'll take a taxi. I'll pay for it out of my allowance," she said.

"Don't be that way," Polly said, and sighed. She stood up

slowly and put her hand at the back of Rebecca's neck. "I'll take you home. We'll stop off for Carvel, how's that?"

"Lousy," Rebecca said. "Just like everything." Turning her back on Polly, she skated to the front of the lobby, where the phones were.

"Henry, let me tell you about that kid," Polly said.

"You're not going to let her take a taxi, are you?" he said.

"At every opportunity, that kid tries to complicate my life. She gets it from her father. Last week he called me up at seven in the morning while he was getting dressed for work. He told me he was wearing a brown-and-white herringbone suit and a yellow shirt." Polly shook her head and began massaging her eyebrows, as if she had a headache. "He wanted to know which tie I thought he should wear."

Henry stared at her, surprised at how mournful she sounded. Under her eyes were delicate crescents of lavender resembling bruises, which he hoped were only makeup. Suddenly, Polly rolled toward him on her skates and wrapped her arms around his back. She rested her head against his shoulder. He started to raise his arms.

"This family," Polly said in a whispery voice, but all he saw was Robert in his herringbone suit, his yellow shirt a size too large for him, a dozen silk ties drooping from the collar.

# Grace

*I*t could break your heart,"
Grace told the television set in a soft, choked voice. She was
watching a morning talk show; today they had on a child with
a rare disease that had prematurely aged him into a little old
man. Eight years old and he was already bald. He had arthritis
and brittle bones, the body of a ninety-year-old. The little
boy's mother was on the show, too. A pleasant-looking woman
in her early thirties, very cheerful. "It could break your
heart," Grace said again, and punched at the button that shut
off the TV.

"Hey," Lucy said. Lucy was her daughter, her only child.
She was twenty-four. Any day now she was going to have a
baby. She had already gone three days past her due date and
was very irritable. To make matters worse, Cliff, the man she
lived with, was several thousand miles away in California. He
was with his mother, who, after a long illness, had recently
fallen into a coma. As soon as he could, he would rush back
East to be with Lucy. But his mother had been in a coma for
almost a week, and there was no telling when she would go.
You can't rush these life-and-death things, Grace had been
saying every time Lucy sighed and insisted that it wasn't fair,

that she'd had about as much as she could take. Things will happen when they happen and no sooner, Grace kept saying in what she hoped was a soothing voice.

"You shouldn't be watching this sort of thing," she told Lucy now. She stood herself directly in front of the TV, as if to protect Lucy from something dangerous behind the blank screen. "The idiot box can be a real comfort at certain times, but a pregnant woman shouldn't concern herself with other people's misery."

Charlotte, Grace's mother, smiled sweetly in Lucy's direction. "I hear you're having a baby," she said. "So what's it going to be?"

"Nobody can keep a secret in this family," Lucy said, winking at Grace. "You confide in a person and in one minute, the whole world knows about it."

"The whole world knows what?" Charlotte said. She was sitting next to Lucy on a brown corduroy couch, a four-hundred-page biography of Eleanor Roosevelt in her lap. She had been carrying the book around for months, taking it with her wherever she went. Once, she'd dropped it into the washing machine, and it took two days on top of the oil burner before it dried out. Charlotte had her lucid moments, but recently there had been periods where she simply sat in a chair with her Eleanor Roosevelt book unopened in her lap, smiling at everyone, or at no one. Sitting there, she seemed happier than she'd ever been, though of course it was a false, empty happiness, the kind that didn't do much good except to keep her out of trouble. But sometimes Grace actually envied her, as she found herself envying Ezra, her chocolate-point Siamese, when he was purring so hard and loud you just couldn't believe anyone on earth could be so utterly blissful. Poor Ezra had been at the wrong place at the wrong time. According to a woman living across the street, whose daughter seemed to know all the details, as a very young kitten Ezra was given a hit of LSD by some college kids in the neighborhood, then abandoned. Grace used to see him lurching around the front of her house like a drunk, and after a few days of watching him, she decided to take him in. Over the years he had managed pretty well, mostly staying indoors, staggering bravely from room to room. After Grace's husband, Alex, had a mild stroke two years ago, Ezra stayed at his side to keep him company while he was home recuperating. Later, when Alex moved out to an apartment in Back Bay, the cat devoted himself to Grace. He got into the habit of sleeping in her bed at night, nestled in the curve of her arm. A very compassionate animal, with good instincts about people.

All her life, Grace had thought of herself in the same way, as someone with a real gift for figuring people out. But when Alex left last year, talking breathlessly about finally having come to grips with the major disappointments in his life, Grace had been completely bewildered. She blamed his departure on all the medication he'd started taking after the stroke. Listening to him race through what sounded like a prepared speech on the necessity of accepting one's own mortality, she decided he was deranged. If, in fact, he wasn't going to live forever, he'd said, he wanted something other than the life he had with her. Grace held on to his hand and told him she understood exactly what he was saying. She let him go, even gave him advice on how to decorate the apartment he'd got for himself on Comm Ave, right near the Common. She drove in from the suburbs and cooked him dinner a few times that first week he was living there, calling him every night around one to say good night before he went to sleep. Finally, he told her very firmly to buzz off. You're driving me crazy, he said. For a quarter of a century, you've slowly been driving me crazy. Grace had called his neurologist and asked about the side effects of the medication he was on. Maybe some forgetfulness, some depression, the doctor said. What about insanity? The doctor laughed. Insanity is a legal term, he told her. Then he said he had to hang up.

Now and then, when she was feeling particularly despairing, Grace found herself wishing she were a widow. A widow got heartfelt sympathy from all quarters. More importantly, she knew for certain it was all over—her husband was buried in the ground, not living it up in a well-kept brownstone in Back Bay, having the time of his life. That was what Alex kept insisting when she last talked with him: he was having the time of his life.

Occasionally, Grace had murderous daydreams about him: Alex with a bullet hole in his temple; with a knife between his ribs; with a pillow pressed tightly against his face. Most probably it was another stroke that would do him in. Those first few days he was in the hospital, he had spoken backwards, struggled hard to remember the word "love." "You you you," he said, and fell silent. And then, triumphantly: "You love I!" Hearing that, she had kissed his hands, his eyes, his throat, so grateful that he had survived. A year later he was on his own in a cozy one-bedroom apartment—a man without a wife, happy as a man in love.

Grace made a point of always dressing well, even though there'd been no one to impress but Charlotte, and now Lucy. Before nine every morning, she was dressed in a pants suit or a casual, flowered-print dress, with a gold bracelet on each wrist, a necklace of tiny ceramic beads that matched her outfit, and plenty of makeup. She felt good, she claimed, knowing she'd made the effort to look decent. Taking pride in one's appearance was a sign that a person cared about living and hadn't given up, she believed. And she hadn't given up. Ever since Alex left, she had been making plans for his return. When he moved back home again, she would throw out their old mattress and get a king-size bed. And a new bedspread with matching drapes, something pastel and flowery. And she and Alex would try hard every night to get into bed together at the same time. Maybe that was part of the problem—she was always going to sleep early, before the eleven o'clock news, while Alex stayed up past one, watching reruns of "Quincy" and "The Rockford Files." These days, Grace hardly slept. With Ezra in her lap, she often read until three in the morning, or half listened to the radio at her bedside while she polished her nails, let them dry, then removed the polish and tried a new color—four or five on the worst nights. She wrote letters to college friends she hadn't seen in ages, reporting that Alex had made a full recovery. Physically, that was. Mentally, he still wasn't himself, but she believed that time would take care of that.

She didn't mention that in the meantime she had a friend, Howard, who took her to the movies on Saturday nights. Howard considered himself far more than a friend, and was dying to sleep with her. No chance in the world of anything like that happening, Grace had told him more than once. Still, it was heartening to have him standing beside her on line at the movies, sitting next to her in the theater, in a booth in a restaurant. It was important to her to feel that she wasn't a woman alone. And sometimes she almost believed it, riding around with Howard in his dark gray Cadillac on a Saturday night. But when he kissed her, as he did at the end of every one of their dates, she felt the full weight of her loss. She'd lost everything. To tell the truth, she'd rather live out her life miserably with Alex than start over again with someone who truly cared about making her happy. She would never admit this to Lucy, or to any of her friends, all of whom would think she was out of her mind. She wasn't out of her mind, she told herself; she was just a woman who loved her husband, mistakenly or not.

Charlotte hadn't had a bath or a shower in nine days. Since Cliff went out to California and Lucy came to stay with them, things had been hectic, and Grace just didn't have the heart to force the issue. But she couldn't put it off any longer: nine days was a disgrace, she felt.

She walked into her mother's bedroom, a small, overheated

room on the first floor that smelled of licorice. Packages of black licorice braids were piled on top of a cherry-wood dresser, along with six-packs of individual-size cans of pineapple juice. These had been bought with what Charlotte mistakenly believed to be her own money, money from her savings account, and she liked to keep them in her room, where she knew they would be safe. Other food that belonged to her was in the refrigerator, labeled with her initials, and not to be touched by anyone else in the house. This was a new system, put into effect several weeks ago with no explanation from Charlotte.

"Bath time," Grace announced. Her mother was standing at the window filing her nails and did not look up. "Shower time," Grace said. "Let's get going."

"Absolutely not," her mother said. She put the nail file sideways in her mouth, and held out her hands, palms up, then turned them over. "I'm as clean as they come," she said. "You've obviously mistaken me for someone else. Maybe your daughter needs a bath. Why don't you go torture her for a while?"

"It's been over a week," Grace said. "It's outrageous. Really."

"Do I smell?" Charlotte said. "Do I smell like a garbage pail?"

Grace wondered if her mother was afraid of the water. "We'll take a shower together, how's that?" she said. "I'll go in first and show you that it doesn't hurt."

"Everything hurts," her mother said. "Or haven't you noticed?" She threw the nail file at Grace's feet. "You rotten kid," she said. "You're the meanest person there ever was."

"If you're not in that bathroom in sixty seconds, there's going to be a war."

"I feel for you, angel, I really do," Charlotte said. "Your husband's gone, never to return, your daughter's going to have a baby, no husband in sight . . . Really, it's been one disaster after another."

"A shower is very relaxing," Grace said. "It eases tension in the muscles. You'll feel like a new person."

"I'm not in the mood to feel like a new person. Anyway, it's still wintertime. I only bathe in warm weather."

Grace grabbed her mother's arm. "Hop to it," she said. "I mean business."

"I understand completely," Charlotte said after a moment, then saluted her.

Down the hall in the bathroom, Grace locked herself in with Charlotte, took off her clothes, and turned on the water for a shower. "I'm waiting," she said to Charlotte. "I'll wait for as long as it takes."

Steam filled the room; her mother stood motionless between the sink and the hamper, fully dressed but barefoot. She waved her hands through the steam. She studied Grace intently, then said, "Do I know you?"

"It's me," Grace said with a sigh. "Me."

"Oh. For a moment there, I thought you were someone else. Well, whoever you are, how *are* you? How are things?"

"Not great."

A smile came to her mother's face. "It's all for the best, angel," she said. "You just keep up the good work." She unlocked the door and backed out of the room, her smile broadening as she moved farther and farther from Grace.


"How long has it been since I've talked to you?" Grace's brother-in-law, Ray, said. "Was it before I came dangerously close to suicide, or after?" They were having lunch, just salad in aluminum-and-plastic containers, and coffee, outside on the Cambridge Common, under a small pin oak. Ray was Alex's much-younger brother, a commercial artist in his late thirties who dressed in jeans and T-shirts with pictures of rock bands on them, and who, in Grace's mind, was about as grown-up as a college student.

"What?" Grace said. She tapped a white plastic fork against

the side of her Styrofoam coffee cup. "What are you talking about?" It was a mild, sweet-smelling day toward the end of March, an ideal day for lunch outdoors. At the center of the Common, a small group of teenage boys were playing electric guitars. Some of them were bare-chested, their shirts tied around their waists. Two shaggy dogs, wearing blue-and-white bandanas at their necks, raced across the grass toward the musicians. Dressed in a bathing suit and high heels, carrying three winter coats over her arm, a street person—old or young, it was impossible to tell—stood still on the cobblestone path that led through the Common. "Man don't want to repent, he want to go to his disco dancing," she said in a deep, scary voice. She switched the coats to her other arm and walked past Grace and Ray. "Miserable scum," she said in a conversational tone.

"Have a nice day," Ray said.

Grace frowned at him. "What's this all about?" she said, annoyed at herself for driving all the way into Cambridge just because Ray had sounded so sad and sweet on the phone this morning when he called to ask if she would meet him for lunch.

"I'm serious," Ray said. "I gave it a great deal of thought. I was just about to slit my wrists with Gillette Super Blues when I suddenly felt compelled to call a suicide hot line. Turns out I called the wrong number, but the person who answered was a Jehovah's Witness, and he took it upon himself to talk me out of it. Great guy. He didn't even try to convert me. Not much, anyway."

Grace laughed. She stacked slices of mushroom on her fork.

"Don't laugh," Ray said. "I'm in therapy now. I'm learning how to live comfortably with rejection."

"Maureen left you again?" Grace said. "I'm sorry." Maureen was the woman he'd been living with on and off for close to ten years. She used to pick out clothing for him at thrift shops, dress him up in faded velvet jackets and bow ties. One time, she'd given his stick-straight, baby-fine hair a home permanent, and he'd walked around for months afterward with hair that wasn't curly at all, just strangely wrinkled. "You're well rid of her," Grace said, "now that I think about it."

"We're still together," Ray said, glaring at her. "She was pregnant, and without letting me know, she went and had an abortion. She doesn't want to marry me or have a family. She just wants to live with me and deny me all the real pleasures of life."

"So what does your therapist think?"

"I told you," Ray said irritably. "I have to learn to live comfortably with rejection."

"How do you do that?"

"I'm working on it."

"I see."

"That's the story," Ray said. "You got it."

"Actually, I have to be getting back soon," Grace said, sneaking a look at her watch. "Lucy could be going into labor at any moment, for all I know."

Ray pulled at the grass at his feet. "My question for you is this: Could you ever see the two of us getting considerably closer than we are now? If I asked you out on a date, for example, what would you think?"

Grace was stunned. All she could do was shake her head. She wouldn't dream of telling him the truth—that the idea of them together struck her as bizarre, even hilarious. What could she possibly want from a man like him—a man who was always attached to some woman or other who managed to get the best of him?

"Goddamn," Ray said. "I can't tell you how disappointed I am. My therapist suggested I have some sexual experiences with someone other than Maureen, and you were at the top of my list."

"You and your therapist sound like a couple of lunatics."

"I'm truly surprised," Ray said. "I figured you'd be an excellent choice—a very attractive woman separated from her husband, stuck in the house with her batty old mother, deeply depressed about all of the above—"

"You, like your brother, are so confused it's painful to listen to you." Grace stood up and brushed bits of grass and earth from the backs of her legs. She looked over at Ray, whose pale, angular face was a younger, slightly softer version of Alex's. "You're going to be forty soon," she said. "Get with it." She left him sitting on the ground, surrounded by the paper and plastic left over from their lunch. "For your information," she called over her shoulder as she moved away from him, "I am not deeply depressed."

She walked with her head down through the lunchtime crowds at Harvard Square, stopping to look up at a gray-haired man in a dirty fisherman's knit sweater who was standing outside the Coop selling long-stemmed plastic flowers. The flowers lit up at the touch of a button hidden in the petals. "Best gift for your loved one," the vendor said, holding out a rose to her. "Only needs one battery. What do you say?"

When Grace shook her head "no," the man sighed and handed her a leaflet advertising a lecture on "Interpersonal Relationships and How They Affect Us." The lecture was being given by a professional psychic who would also speak on self-analysis through astrology.

"Maybe next year," Grace said, and slapped the paper into the vendor's hand.

"You ladies," the man said darkly. "You think you know everything."

At home, Lucy was waiting for her at the front door, her face framed in the small rectangle of glass set in at eye level. She was squeezing her hands together; her face was dead-white.

"What?" Grace said. "What is it?" Her first thought was that Cliff's mother had died: she'd been sick for so long, and now, finally, it was over. Poor Cliff. But it's the natural order of things, she wanted to say, as if there were any comfort in that. Sooner or later, every child lost his parents. Better that than the other way around, she could say.

"Oh Lucy," she murmured, moving closer and reaching for her. With Lucy's huge stomach in the way, it was more of a collision than an embrace.

"Look," Lucy said, and stretched out her arm. "Look at this."

Grace looked; there were goose bumps along Lucy's small, very white arm.

*"Look,"* Lucy said again. *"Pay attention!"*

Now she saw what Lucy was gesturing toward: the living room and dining room were empty of furniture. The piano was gone, the coffee table, a pair of armchairs, the breakfront, the couch, the dining room table and chairs. Everything. So the house was robbed. "What else did they take?" she asked in a faint voice. For some reason, she didn't care as much as she imagined she was supposed to. The living room, she noticed, looked better without all that dark, heavy furniture she'd been so crazy for when she was first married. She could see herself having guests over, having them sit on the floor in a circle, balancing plates of food in their laps. Maybe she wouldn't even bother to replace any of the stolen things—the idea of living in a house full of empty rooms suddenly appealed to her.

"You're not getting it right," Lucy said. "The window washers were here today. You forgot to tell me they were coming, incidentally. Anyway, two men came with all their equipment and did a lousy job. I don't know what their problem was, but the windows didn't look clean at all. After they left, I called the company they worked for and told the boss they'd screwed up. So they came back. And moved all the furniture and went home." She pointed upstairs. "Come on up."

In the hallway, blocking the entrance to the second-floor bathroom, was the piano. The master bedroom had the couch in it, and the breakfront. A heavy armchair sat on top of the bed. Ezra was asleep on the velvet cushion, his chin lowered onto his front paws. "Grandma and I were out while they were working, sitting on lawn chairs in the backyard. It was such a beautiful day, it seemed stupid to stay indoors." Lucy looked at her. "None of this is my fault, is it?"

"Forget about that," Grace said.

"They must have just sauntered out the front door when they were finished, very pleased with themselves, I'm sure."

"Who were they?" Grace asked as she struggled to lift the armchair off the bed. Ezra jumped awkwardly to the floor and landed on Grace's foot, where he stayed until she shook him off. "What did they look like?"

"Two young guys with tattooed arms. Neither of them used deodorant."

"Did you call the police?"

Lucy made a short, dry sound presumably meant to be a laugh. "And say what? Two men rearranged the furniture for us while I was sunning myself in the backyard? I called Daddy at the office, though. I was so spaced out, I had to call someone. He's on his way over."

"Thanks a lot," Grace said. "Thanks for everything."

"I thought he could help us move the furniture back. I'm sorry."

"I don't know." It had been so long since she'd seen him she was getting panicky just thinking about him being there in the house. And after he left, she wouldn't know which end was up. She'd awaken tomorrow morning newly disheartened not to find him there next to her. "No," she told Lucy. "The rule is, he's not to set foot in this house until he's ready to come back for good."

"Don't hold your breath," Lucy said. "Who knows what kind of weird plans he's making?"

"You're supposed to be a comfort to me in my old age," Grace said. "You're not supposed to be the one to put unspeakable thoughts into my head."

The doorbell was ringing, one urgent ring on top of another. Grace rushed downstairs. On the front stoop was Janet, the woman who was renting the house next door. Janet was divorced and lived with her lover, a member of the local police force, and her ten-year-old son, who was always riding his bicycle on Grace's lawn, dressed in summer clothes, no matter what the season. Standing behind Janet was Charlotte, looking down at the concrete, her hands clasped behind her back.

"To be brief," Janet said, "I found your mother rummaging through my garbage pails." Janet was wearing a short white terry-cloth bathrobe and was barefoot. Grace could see the police car parked out in front of the house: probably they'd been in the middle of an afternoon quickie when they heard the sound of garbage cans crashing against aluminum siding.

"I'm sorry," Grace said, and stepped outside to lead her mother back into the house.

"She took a light bulb, a little pocket mirror, and some tinfoil. I made her put everything back, of course. You probably ought to wash her hands."

"I'm sorry," Grace said again. "This is something new with her, as far as I know."

"Maybe," Janet said, "you ought to keep a tighter leash on her."

Grace, who didn't fight with neighbors, ever, said, "Your son is riding on my lawn every time I look out the window. And he's never dressed properly. Doesn't he have a winter coat?"

"Listen, I don't have time for this nonsense," Janet said. "And if you don't like Sean riding on your grass, you have my permission to hit him over the head with your shoe the next time you catch him doing it."

Grace watched through the storm door as Janet crossed the lawn and disappeared inside her house. Then she turned to her mother and said, "Let's get those hands washed, please."

"Really," Charlotte said, "sometimes I wonder what I'd do without you and your infinite wisdom."

"How about telling me what you were hoping to accomplish going through her garbage?"

"The living room looks nice," Charlotte said. "Who's your decorator?" In the kitchen, she washed her hands with lemon-scented dishwashing detergent. She was whistling something that sounded like "Country Gardens."

Grace said, "I'd like to see a little remorse in you, Ma. Some sign of deeply felt guilt."

"Can't you call me Charlotte? In all the years we've known each other, you've never once called me by my right name," her mother complained.

Lucy was preparing a peanut-butter-and-marshmallow-cream sandwich for herself at the table. She worked over it a long time, annoying Grace with the way she drew pictures in the peanut butter with her knife. Finally she folded the sandwich in half and took a small bite.

"That is an offensive sight, that sandwich," Grace said. "Who taught you to eat like that?"

"Could I have a glass of milk?"

Grace went to the refrigerator; when she turned back to the table, Alex was in the kitchen doorway, a Yorkshire terrier at his feet. The terrier had on a tan trench coat with leather buckles at the shoulders—as spiffy a raincoat as *she'd* ever had, Grace thought.

"How do you do," Alex said. He took the carton of milk from her and held her fingertips in his hand.

"Is the doorbell broken?" Grace said. "Or didn't you notice we had one?"

"It didn't even cross my mind that I was expected to ring the bell," Alex said. "Please forgive the outrageous breach of etiquette."

"Since when are you a dog-lover?" Lucy asked him.

"That's a very impressive raincoat," Grace said, "if you happen to like dogs in raincoats."

"Say hello to Chuck, everyone." Alex crouched down and patted the dog on the head, where two tortoiseshell barrettes held Chuck's hair in tiny pigtails. Alex explained that he'd been taking care of him while the friend who owned him was out of town.

"Which friend is that?" Lucy said. She lifted the milk carton to her mouth and took a swallow. Grace rolled her eyes at her. "You forgot to give me a glass," Lucy said. "And anyway, it's all in the family."

"Some of us are more in the family than others," Grace said. "Some of us are merely on the periphery."

"She's an art teacher," Alex said. "Teaches little kids how to paste raw macaroni on construction paper and stuff like that."

"If her dog pees on my kitchen floor, you're in big trouble' Grace said. She looked hard at Alex; without the beard he'd worn since he'd had the stroke, his face looked pale, and—amazingly—unfamiliar. He must have begun dyeing his hair; there wasn't much gray in it anymore, except at the sideburns. A long time ago, when they'd been married only a short while, Grace sometimes tried to imagine him old, his hands spotted and a little shaky, his hair bright silver. Of course she failed to imagine it—it was impossible that he would ever be anything other than what he was then; that either of them would ever be any different, or feel any differently toward one another. Who would have guessed then that this impossible place and moment was precisely where they were headed, that every one of the thousands of days they would spend together would just be bringing them one day closer to this?

It was a mystery to Grace that Alex had lost interest in who she was, in what she was thinking. He was paying very little attention to her now that they were in the same room. It was Lucy he wanted to hear from—he was squatting at her feet, asking her how she felt, holding her hand between his own.

Grace walked away, picked up a dustcloth lying on a bookcase and drifted from room to room, collecting dust wherever she could, her mind so fixed on what she was doing it was as if she were on a treasure hunt, looking for something precious

Alex wouldn't let go of Lucy's hand. "Tell me," he said. "Is your mother serious about that guy or what?"

Lucy thought of Howard, his big feet in expensive shoes, his large manicured hands; his mouth nearly always set in a smile, letting you see his beautiful capped teeth. "I can't see it," she said. She looked at her father. "I can't see any of it."

"Goddamnit," Alex said, standing up and then slamming a fist into the open palm of his hand. "I know what it is. She'll love me forever just to be uncooperative."

"You don't love her?" Lucy said in a whisper.

"Love," Alex said, and hung his head. "You I love, your baby I'll love . . . your mother I endure. Endured," he corrected himself. "Listen, you heard it straight from the horse's mouth. There's nothing to misinterpret. You see before you a happy man. I'm away from your mother and it's a pleasure. Every minute of it."

"What's a pleasure?" Charlotte said, smiling. She was still at the table, eating a bowl of cottage cheese and bright yellow canned pineapple rings. "If something's a pleasure, I want to know about it."

"He doesn't know what he's talking about," Lucy said.

"Suit yourself," Alex said. "I have a backache. If you two ladies will excuse me, I'm going to lie down for a while."

"I'm leaving too," Charlotte said. "Good-bye and good luck."

"What kind of backache?" Lucy said as Charlotte wandered out. She wasn't going to let her father disappear like that. She didn't believe he had a backache, only that he was accustomed to doing what he pleased, and right now it pleased him to be alone. When she was growing up in her parents' house, her father used to go into hiding immediately after dinner every night. He would retreat into his bedroom with a box of Mister Salty pretzels and a murder mystery or a book on gardening from the library, surfacing in the kitchen every hour or so for a coffee mug full of club soda. All this time her mother would have been on the phone, talking quietly to her cousin, Cynthia. Cynthia lived three blocks away and was Grace's best friend. They never went anywhere together, though, because

Cynthia was afraid to leave the house. Grace did all her shopping for her and went to see all the movies Cynthia would have seen if she could have made it out the door. Grace reported back to her on every one of them, and on anything else she thought Cynthia might have wanted to know about. Cynthia had no children; she'd given birth to a baby who'd strangled on the umbilical cord, and a year and a half later she divorced her husband. In Lucy's mind there had been a connection between the baby and Cynthia's never leaving the house, but it wasn't talked about and she never knew if she was right or not. Her father thought Cynthia was a self-indulgent pain-in-the-ass and had said so whenever he had the opportunity. Have a little compassion, Grace kept telling him as she reached for the phone and another endless conversation that drove Alex into the bedroom for the night. As it turned out, he knew what he was talking about. Eventually Cynthia pulled herself together, moved to Miami Beach, remarried, and was never heard from again except at Christmastime, when she would send the family a small crate of oranges and grapefruits without even a card inside. Grace was devastated. You eat that stuff and you're as wacked-out as she is, Alex said every Christmas, scowling at the crate that sat unopened on the kitchen table. Lucy and her mother had eaten the oranges and grapefruits anyway, because, as Grace said, it was foolish to throw out perfectly good food like that, even if it got you depressed just looking at it.

Years after Cynthia's departure, Alex was still hiding out with his pretzels and library books, even though Grace was no longer anchored to the phone by the weight of her compassion.

"A tension backache is what I've got," Alex said.

"Look at that," Lucy said. She pointed to the gleaming circle on the floor where Chuck had just peed.

"I knew it," Alex said. "I knew that dog was going to do his thing on your mother's floor. Truthfully, I'm fed up with the little runt. You know what he eats for dinner? Baby-size hamburgers that I have to fry up in a pan for him every night."

"Can I ask you why he's wearing a raincoat on a day like this?"

Alex was mopping up the puddle with paper towels as Chuck ran under the table. "He just got over some kind of virus, and his ah . . . mistress told me to make sure he's properly dressed whenever he goes out."

"The art teacher," Lucy said. "Is that the mistress you're referring to?"

"Cut it out, will you," Alex said. "She's not my mistress. At least she's not anymore. We used to sleep together, but that didn't work out too well."

Lucy said, "I don't care what you do in your spare time. You can hang by your toes from a curtain rod, for all I care."

"You do care. You say you don't, but obviously you do. I know what's going on. You want me to stick to your mother like glue and live a life of unmitigated aggravation. Well, I have news for you, it's not going to happen."

Lucy started to cry. "I'm crying because you make me hate you," she said after a while.

"It's all right," Alex said, smiling at her. "Since I've been in therapy I've learned how to cry, and it's really all right. I find myself crying a couple of times a week these days, sometimes more. There's no point in holding back, that's the way I see it."

"Drop dead."

"I understand," Alex said. The smile had faded from his face. "Do you know where your mother keeps the mop? I think I'll do her a favor and wash the floor."


Grace was looking at herself in the large mahogany-framed mirror over her dresser. Greenish-gray eyes, smooth skin, too much makeup everywhere. She dipped a tissue into a jar of Vaseline, streaked it across her eyes. She couldn't see a thing now. Downstairs, the house was still. Perhaps she was alone;

perhaps it was just that Alex and Lucy were arguing in whispers. Lucy, Grace knew, was furious with him for dumping her. She'd thought their marriage was a sure thing, as safe as a boat anchored in quiet waters. There's no such thing as a sure thing anymore, Grace had tried to tell her. Then she told Lucy not to listen to her, because whatever had happened during the past year had made her doubt everything she said and did. She wasn't to be trusted anymore; all her good sense had gone straight out the window. For one full year she'd been in a state of shock. What she needed to do, of course, was just lie back and let herself be convinced there was more to life than love. Our life together is a big bore, plain and simple, Alex had explained to her over the phone, a few days after he made his move. We've been on automatic pilot for so long we never realized we've gone nowhere. Nowhere.

Grace told him that was very interesting; she presumed his idea of somewhere was a grass hut in Tahiti. Sounds good to me, Alex had said, but Back Bay was as far as he'd been willing to go. And that was a solid point in her favor, Grace thought, the fact that he'd stayed so close to home.

The telephone in her bedroom began to ring. Wiping her eyes with fresh tissues, Grace blinked until things came back into focus. She went to the phone, hoping it was Howard calling to cancel twenty-four hours in advance. Howard was always a little too eager to please for her taste. She'd been giving him a hard time lately, turning weepy in the front seat of his car after they'd kissed and his hands began searching for buttons in the dark. He understood why she was crying, understood that no matter how hard he tried, no matter what he did, it just couldn't do the trick for her. He knew it wasn't working. But he was as patient as could be, and full of hope. He waited quietly for her to stop crying, and then he told her that, as always, he'd had a wonderful time. He walked Grace to her door, promising that next Saturday would be even better. A better movie? A better restaurant? He didn't say. He only knew that next time around would be better. Grace shrugged her shoulders slightly and had to smile at him, because it was hard not to be agreeable in the face of all that sweet optimism.

On the phone, a voice asked, "Is my brother there?"

"Who's your brother?" Grace said.

"I only have one brother, and he's married to you."

"If you're calling to apologize, Ray, you've already started off on the wrong foot."

"Where's Alex?"

"I don't know. He was here, but he may have left. What do you want?"

"Family business," Ray said. "You wouldn't be interested." He made a whistling sound through his teeth, then turned it into a sigh. "You're an exceptionally attractive woman," he said sadly. "I recognized that fact even when I was in high school and you were an old married lady. I don't know why Alex did what he did, but then again, he's always been something of an asshole—"

"Stop right there," Grace said.

"This is as close to an apology as I'm willing to give," Ray said. "Let me finish."

"Leave your name and number, and the doctor will get back to you," Grace said, and then she hung up. She made her way downstairs, but no one was around except her mother, who was sitting in the kitchen smoking a cigarette.

"Where did you get that?" Grace asked her. "Who gave you a cigarette?"

"None of your business."

Grace took the cigarette away from her mother and ran it under the faucet. "There's no smoking in this house," she said. From the bottom shelf of the cabinet over the dishwasher, she removed a small plastic bowl full of matchbooks. Standing on her toes, she shoved the bowl to the back of the top shelf, saying, "All I need is for you to burn the house down."

"I'm so mad, I could kill," Charlotte said. "Someone ate

almost an entire container of cottage cheese that belonged to me personally."

"Really?" Grace said. "Remind me to make sure the guilty party is severely punished."

Charlotte grabbed Grace's sleeve. "Your daughter is a whore," she said. Her eyes glittered with excitement. "I'm pretty sure I saw her on the street soliciting, right in front of this house. What are you going to do about it?"

"I'm thinking," Grace said. "Give me a minute."

"Well, I've been watching her like a hawk and I have to say I don't like what I see. It's unbecoming for a college graduate to behave like that, especially in broad daylight."

Grace was silent, wondering if Alex would stay for dinner, if Lucy would give birth to her baby tonight, if the three of them would race off to the hospital, a family on an extraordinary midnight expedition; the three of them holding tight to each other in the hospital corridors, Lucy in the middle, she and Alex on either side; a family who would not let go, no matter what.

"Well," Charlotte said, "it's up to you. You're the mother."

Alex sat at the piano outside the second-floor bathroom playing "Night and Day." From there he went into "Begin the Beguine" and then "In the Still of the Night." The music was impossibly romantic; watching him, the confident way his hands came down on the keys, the slope of his shoulders as he bent in toward the music, watching him from the slightest distance, Grace felt out of control. Her arm shot out, her finger traveled along a single pinstripe of his shirt, grazing the bumps of his spine. Under her breath she said, "Excuse me," and took her hand away, but Alex went on playing, unaware that she'd trespassed.

"I miss having a piano," he said when he finished. "Especially at night, sometimes, when there doesn't seem to be anything much to do . . ."

"It's all yours," Grace said. "Rent a U-Haul and take it out of here. Nobody plays it here—it's just another piece of furniture, as far as I'm concerned."

"I don't know. I guess I'd have to check with my lawyer first," Alex said, sounding apologetic.

"Lawyer." She was tired suddenly, and sat down next to Alex on the piano bench. He looked at the keys for a while, then lifted her arm by the wrist and studied her hand. "You see before you the hand of a middle-aged person," Grace said, wiggling her fingers to disguise their trembling. "Someone who remembers V-E Day and life before Saran Wrap."

"I have to go," Alex said. He dropped her hand somewhere around middle C. "I have to get home."

"You have to feed the dog."

"Among other things."

After a while Grace said, "Are you ever lonely? You don't have to be embarrassed—your secrets are always safe with me," she joked. She smiled at Alex, but he didn't smile back.

"I have no great compulsion to discuss my private life with you," he said.

"Why?" Grace said. "Why does everything have to be classified information?"

"Because that's the way I prefer it."

"Even if we're not living together anymore," Grace told him, "I have to feel as if I know what you're doing. We don't talk to each other for months, and all that time I'm going crazy trying to imagine your life."

"Oh Jesus," Alex said. "Don't waste your time."

Grace stood up, pressing her fingers against the piano keys for balance. "I have to make dinner for my family," she announced.

"It's a very simple thing," Alex said. "I just want to be left alone."

"You won't be staying for dinner, then."

"I'm on my way out," Alex said, though he still hadn't moved from the piano bench. He played a few bars of something Grace didn't recognize, then stopped. "You want to know about my life," he said, swinging his legs over the bench so that he was facing her. "Weekend mornings I jog through the Common a few times. I usually bake one of those Duncan Hines cakes after I get back. I have one small piece a day and it lasts about a week, when it's time to make another one. Now that I'm a city boy, there's not much gardening I can do except what I can grow in my window box. That's the saddest thing of all to me. But I'm content; I like the silence I come home to every night. The perfect silence."

"You like the silence," Grace said. So all those years she'd been married to someone who only wanted to be alone with his silence. "Did you ever think about spending the rest of your life in the public library? You could just sit around soaking up the perfect silence all day."

"I don't enjoy talking with you anymore," Alex said. He started down the stairs. "Or maybe it's just this house. I shouldn't spend time here, I suppose. What good can it do?"

"You were invited here to help move the furniture back."

"Me?" Alex said. "Can't you wait for Cliff to get back?"

"Apparently I'll have to," Grace said without looking up at him. She must have looked pretty miserable; when she raised her head, Alex had his thumbs hooked through his belt loops and was doing a soundless tap dance on the living room carpet. Then both arms swung to the left and to the right, as if he were doing the Charleston. He made it all the way to the front door without missing a step.

At the door she said, "What grace, what style. You danced your way right into my heart, as they say."

"A dangerous place," Alex said quietly. She thought he was going to say more, but he was silent. Neither of them said good-bye. Grace sank face down on the carpet with her eyes closed, listening for the sound of his car pulling away. But then he was back, standing in the foyer, looking embarrassed. "I forgot the damn dog," he said. "It just occurred to me I don't even know where he is. What if he's lost?"

Grace stayed where she was. "Tough break for the macaroni lady."

"Help me," Alex said. "Please."

"We're no longer allies," she reminded him. "We're adversaries."

"Don't," Alex said. "Don't be so quick to say things like
that."

"We're not adversaries?"

"I'm not exactly sure *what* we are," he said, and that was
good enough for her. Together they searched for the dog,
who turned up in the backyard dozing under a crab apple tree,
his raincoat wrinkled and streaked with dirt.


Howard wanted Grace to meet his sons. He sounded very
excited when he phoned early in the morning to tell her "the
boys," as he called them, were in town for the weekend.
"We'll all go out for dinner," he said. "The boys are just dying
to meet you." The boys were identical twins named William
and Anthony. They were both in law school in Chicago, and
Howard was very proud of them. When his wife had left him,
William and Anthony were still living at home, and according
to Howard, they'd saved his life. That summer they took him
to baseball games at Fenway, to outdoor concerts along the
Charles, to dozens of out-of-the-way restaurants—Vietnamese,
Hungarian, Brazilian, any kind you could imagine. We were
inseparable, Howard told Grace earnestly. Triplets who went
almost everywhere together. His wife went to the Bahamas
with her beloved, a rich man who owned a company that made
false teeth. For years before she left, Howard's wife had been
arriving home late every Thursday night, the night all the
department stores were open until nine. She rarely bought
anything, but she never got home before eleven, sometimes
much later. Eventually Howard understood that she hadn't
been spending much time shopping. He developed colitis. He
lost weight, thirty-five pounds in one year. He called his wife

a whore right to her face, but it didn't make much of an impression on her. When she left, it was with department-store shopping bags full of cruisewear her lover had bought her for their trip.

Howard insisted that he neither forgave nor forgot. But at least his colitis was under control, he told Grace.

She wasn't all that keen on meeting the boys, mostly because it sounded like a serious and formal step, one step before the engagement ring in the small velvet box. But not wanting to hurt Howard's feelings and not wanting to leave Charlotte and Lucy alone for the night, she invited everyone over for dinner. "Are you sure?" Howard asked her. "Are you sure you want to go to all that trouble?" He couldn't quite believe she was finally offering him something that seemed to show she had some real affection for him after all. And she did feel affection for him, even if it stemmed from gratitude and little else. It was even possible that if she'd wanted to fall in love, Howard would have done just fine. If she'd wanted it badly enough, probably almost anyone at all would have done the trick. She'd seen it happen. When the time and place were right, people would let themselves drift toward love. Like Lucy. Two years out of college, a couple of disappointing jobs, and she was ready to let things happen. Cliff, who'd dropped out of medical school twice, and also out of a doctoral program in English, obviously needed something, though a baby seemed an unlikely choice. (It would be a small relief to her if they got their act together and decided to get married, but Grace wasn't counting on it.)

When she told Lucy they were having company over for dinner, Lucy said, "Oh boy, Howard and the twins. Sounds like a New Wave group." Grace stared at her. "You know," Lucy said, but didn't explain further. She was watching television again, a show where teenagers, mostly black, were dancing to canned disco music. Maybe it was a dance contest, maybe they were doing it strictly for pleasure; it was impossible to tell.

"I had to invite them," Grace said, feeling defensive. "There just didn't seem to be any way out of it."

"There's always a way out," Lucy said. "You just have to know how to get tough."

"I know all about that," Grace said. "Did I tell you I'm planning to write a book called *How to Get Tough with Yourself and Others*?" She watched the dancers whirling on the screen. After a while she shut her eyes. "Your father's having second thoughts," she said. She hadn't felt confident saying it, but once said, it seemed true enough.

"We don't talk much," Lucy said. "I wouldn't know."

"You're always so angry with him. What does he say to you?"

"Garbage," Lucy said. "That and more garbage." She lifted her feet off the hassock they were resting on and reached for the newspaper. She studied the TV listings, then folded the paper and spun it across the room like a Frisbee. It hit a laminated diploma hanging on the paneled wall and knocked it to the floor. "It's never going to end," she said. "My kid will be in college and I'll still be listening to the same old bullshit."

Grace picked up the diploma. One of its edges was badly chipped. She hung it back on the wall anyway. "You're not the first person in the world to have a baby," she said. "Take it easy."

"I've been here a week and it seems like a year," Lucy said. "I look at my watch a hundred times a day. I try to guess what time it is and I'm always right. Ask me what time it is so I can demonstrate my talent."

Wanting to do something for her daughter but not knowing what, Grace couldn't get beyond the obvious; that in a day or two, or possibly an hour or two, Lucy would have what she wanted; it was inevitable. That alone should have kept her going—the knowledge that all she had to do was be patient. Grace wondered how she would feel then, hearing the news from Lucy. She'd call Alex, of course, and over the phone she'd listen for the catch in his voice, evidence that

what happened to his family mattered to him. But what if it
didn't? He could just mumble congratulations and thank her
for calling. Hang up at the earliest possible moment so she
didn't get the idea that in his eyes they were, in fact, a family. If he wanted to be left alone, as he said, maybe she
should take him at his word and leave him to savor the silence of his apartment. And if that was what made him happiest, he was a lost cause. Forget the medication—there was
only so much you could blame on that—her husband was
contemptible. She hated him. She wanted nothing further to
do with him. She'd never truly hated anyone; this was something remarkable. She was buoyant, weightless; she could
have floated through the roof and beyond. She no longer
loved him, because how could you love a man you found
contemptible? With a little effort, you could almost feel
sorry for a man like that, a man who'd let his family slip
through his fingers.

"I'm ten months' pregnant and I'm losing my mind," Lucy
was saying. "Is that it?"

"I'm here," Charlotte said in a voice that startled Grace and
Lucy; neither of them had heard her come into the room.
"How much longer do I have to wait here before someone
acknowledges my presence?" She was wearing a maroon wool
bathrobe and a pair of men's leather slippers. There was a
towel over her shoulder and a book under her arm. "Don't
my footsteps make noise anymore?" she said.

"I'll go and fill the tub for you, if you're sure you're ready,"
Grace said.

"I'm a man of my word. I've always been a man of my
word," Charlotte said cheerfully.

"I'm sure you are." Grace steered her across the hall to the
bathroom. Her mother kicked at the frosted glass of the
shower door with the toe of her slipper. "Now, just one
minute," she said. "I was promised a bath. How can I take a
bath in there?" she said, shaking her head at the stall shower.

"You can't. We can't get into the upstairs bathroom because

the piano's in front of the door. You'll have to take a shower down here."

"You're coming in with me, then."

"We'll compromise," Grace said, because she'd already taken one shower this morning and had no intention of taking another. "I'll get the water just the way you want it and all you'll have to do is hop in. I'll stay right here and give you moral support. I'll be at the sidelines cheering you on."

"I can't do it without you," Charlotte said. "Do you understand what I'm saying?"

She understood that she had no choice, that her mother would not back down, would probably never back down from anything. If she were to fight her mother, it would be the pure egoism of old age she'd be up against—or at least her mother's old age. What if it was in the genes, this outrageous self-centeredness. She'd want Lucy to shoot her in the head. Do your old mother a favor and shoot her in the head. *If you don't like my son riding on your grass, you have my permission to shoot him in the head.* Jackass. She had no proof, but she suspected that Janet kicked her son out of the house every time she and her lover were in the mood. She'd even seen the little boy, Sean, riding his bicycle in the rain, waiting for the all-clear signal from his mother, probably.

Charlotte said, "I'm taking off my bathrobe now, if that's all right with you, sweetie pie."

Grace ran the water until she was satisfied the temperature was perfect. "Go on in," she said. "It's all set."

"You first," her mother said.

"How do I know this isn't a trick?"

"I'm all out of tricks today." Charlotte smiled at her, asked her to hurry up. Grace undressed quickly and stepped under the water. Miraculously, her mother followed her into the stall. But she was standing against the shiny tiled wall, looking bewildered, one arm covering her breasts. She was a large, long-limbed woman, hardly diminished by age. She'd always been bigger than Grace. What was she so fearful of, hanging back from the water with that dazed look?

"Charlotte," Grace said, since that was what her mother wanted to hear. She took a few steps toward her and, with her hands at her mother's waist, eased her under the spray. She soaped up her mother's back, then carefully turned her around. Her mother was crying, weeping into the water in a terrible voice, as if she were in pain. Grace soaped up her neck and her arms; she could not bring herself to touch the fallen breasts. She thought, suddenly, that this would be her body— skin hanging loosely from bone, thin white hair with that strange yellow cast—that what was impossibly foreign had to become familiar, even well loved.

She moved past her mother and shut off the water.

"How could you do this to me?" Charlotte said, stamping her foot against the shower floor. "I no longer have any faith in you whatsoever."

"Just let me get you a towel."

"I want nothing further to do with you."

"Let me dry you off."

"Get lost," Charlotte said as Grace patted her dry with a huge royal blue bath sheet that Alex always kept for himself. "You misled me," her mother said. "You promised me one thing and gave me another."

"How about some baby powder?"

"You're persona non grata in this house. You no longer exist," Charlotte said.

"There's roast beef for dinner tonight," Grace said. "We're having company over, Howard and his sons. I just wanted to warn you in advance." She smoothed powder across her mother's shoulders and helped her into her bathrobe.

"You're a ghost," her mother said. "You have no voice. I can't hear a word you're saying." She pushed past Grace and then was out the door, letting in a rush of ice-cold air that left Grace shaking.

Like a diver rising to the surface, she felt herself traveling toward sunlight from someplace deep and soundless.

"He's flying home tomorrow," she heard Lucy saying. "It wasn't my idea, but it's true that there's really nothing he can do for his mother, anyway."

"How long have I been sleeping?" Grace said. She sat up and eased herself to the edge of the bed, dangling her feet over the side. They're letting me dangle, she remembered Alex saying in his slightly slurred speech over the phone a few days after his stroke. They're letting me dangle my legs from the bed, like a little boy fishing from a pier. She'd cried when she'd heard that, picturing his long white feet swinging slowly above the hospital floor.

"You were out a long time. What happened to you?"

"Are you all right?" Grace said. "I mean, is Cliff all right?"

Lucy lowered herself to the carpet and sat with her back against the closet door. "At first, on the phone, he was hardly saying anything at all, and then he started to tell stories I'd heard a long time ago, about how his father used to have terrible arguments with his mother sometimes and afterward would wake up Cliff and his sister, yank them out of bed and hit them with his fists, just to make himself feel better, apparently. His mother would hide in the bathroom, behind the shower curtain, until it was all over. That's all he can talk about now, about how his mother stayed behind the shower curtain."

Grace was close to tears; for Cliff, an almost son-in-law, sweet and cheerful, with a beer belly she always had the urge to poke; for his mother, whom she'd never met or even spoken to. She crossed the room and settled on the floor beside Lucy, saying, "It's too much." She wrapped her arms around Lucy's shoulders, hid her face in Lucy's hair. "After a while, you just have to pretend that you're not hearing anything anymore, that nothing's getting through to you. Pretty soon you're happy as a lark."

"In seventh heaven."

Grace sighed into Lucy's hair, warming herself. "Why not," she said.

Crowded together behind Howard in the foyer, their reddish-blond hair shining in the bright overhead light, William and Anthony kept their eyes on Grace. They were both broad-shouldered giants way over six feet tall, and both were dressed in dark turtlenecks and camel's-hair blazers. Except for the beard one of them was growing, they looked remarkably alike.

"I'm the one generally considered to be nicer," the bearded one said, handing Grace a bottle of wine with a red ribbon around its neck. "I'm Anthony."

"I'm the older one," William said. "By six minutes." In his hand was a single plastic rose, its stem wrapped in aluminum foil. "Wait till you see this," he said. "It lights up in the dark and can be fully enjoyed either at home or in the office."

"He's also the obnoxious one," Anthony said. "That's the easiest way to tell us apart."

Howard rested his hands at the sides of Grace's neck and kissed her cheek. His breath smelled unmistakably of alcohol, which surprised her, since she'd never seen him drink anything stronger than tea. "So what do you think?" he said.

"She's probably thinking that we were valuable additions to our high-school and college basketball teams," Anthony said. "Unfortunately, possessing neither speed nor strength, we were totally useless."

"Funny," William said, turning his head toward the living room, "I once had a fiancée who shared a similar philosophy of home decorating. Her apartment was basically empty except for some straw mats. You sat on them, ate on them, slept on them—"

"You big jerk," his brother said.

"What happened here?" Howard said. "Did something happen?"

Grace didn't have the energy for a detailed explanation and said only that there had been a misunderstanding with some workmen and that all the furniture was upstairs.

"Need some help?" the twins said at the same time. They took off their blazers, hung them over the banister, and pushed up the sleeves of their sweaters.

"Wait a minute," Howard said. "Who's the one with the hernia?"

"We both are," Anthony said, "but that was fifteen years ago."

"Now, here's an idea," Howard said. "We could eat on the floor. We could sit on straw mats in the lotus position and contemplate our food. Did you boys know," he said, "that in the last year of our marriage your mother was deeply involved in yoga?"

"Dad."

"Three frozen banana daiquiris and he doesn't know whether he's coming or going," William said.

"He hates the taste of anything alcoholic," Anthony said to Grace. "So he orders baby drinks and embarrasses us all."

"He was nervous about coming here," Grace said. "Is that what it is?"

Howard was sitting on the floor where the couch used to be. "I'm a little dizzy," he said. "I need a minute or two to get my bearings and I'll be fine."

Lucy came down the stairs just as the twins were going up. She introduced herself, holding onto the banister with her right hand and shaking hands with her left.

"Don't be shy," William said. "If you need a lift to the hospital, we'd be happy to drive you over."

"He means well," Anthony said. "He's a smart-ass, but he'd give you the proverbial shirt off his back anytime."

"Both my boys are good boys," Howard called up to Lucy. "They mother me like you wouldn't believe. They tried their hardest to keep me from that third daiquiri, in fact, and if I'd had the good sense to listen to them, I wouldn't be sitting on the floor now, trying desperately to get my bearings."

"Nice to see you, Howard," Lucy said.

"I'm mortified. I'd planned to be in top form tonight, and here I am on the floor."

"There's a couch and chairs for you, but they're upstairs," Lucy said. "So you're not entirely to blame."

"Your mother tells me you're having a baby," Howard said after a moment. "That's certainly exciting." His knees were drawn up under his chin, and his eyes were closed.

Lucy was silent.

"I'm very enthusiastic about babies," Howard continued. "They're like little animals at first, very uncivilized, but if you bring them up to be human beings, it can be very satisfying. Actually, when you think about it, there's a lot to be said for human beings."

From the top of the stairs, the twins snickered. "You're really onto something now, Dad," one of them said. "Go with it."

"We're all ears," the other one said.

Grace asked them to go on up to the spare bedroom. "Just bring down the dining room table and chairs, and we can all sit down to dinner." These were the sons Howard was so proud of, the sons he would always love. Lucky for her she wasn't in love with him; if she were, she would have been despairing now. Not being in love with him actually had its advantages—something that hadn't occurred to her before. It was an exhilarating thought, knowing that William and Anthony were nothing to her; that dinner was all she had to give them.

In the kitchen, she sliced through the roast beef with an electric knife. Her mother was at the table, eating from a box of Stoned Wheat Thins and reading her Eleanor Roosevelt book. "An extraordinary woman," Charlotte said. "And how."

"I take it you're not angry at me anymore."

"Forgive and forget," Charlotte said matter-of-factly. "Who are those extremely tall people out there?"

"Those are Howard's sons."

"How'd they get so big?"

"Vitamins," Grace said. "And I presume they ate all their vegetables. Are you joining us for dinner?"

"When's Lucy having her baby? She's big as a house."

Grace transferred the meat from the carving board to a platter and took a pitcher of ice water and a glass salad bowl from the refrigerator. She felt like someone's wife, a woman forced to entertain people from her husband's office or weekly poker game. She hadn't enjoyed preparing food since Alex moved out, hadn't even bothered to put a tablecloth over the table since last spring. With her own small meals taken at odd moments and her mother eating crackers from a box and cottage cheese in a turquoise Melmac bowl day after day, there'd been no reason to mark their meals as occasions, to pretend, with linen and dishes from a matched set, that food was a pleasure to be shared. What was there to take pleasure in now, to look forward to taking pleasure in? Alex's return. Lucy's baby. The resumption of an orderly life, a life she could make some sense of. Meals she could set a clock by, sleep that came easily. A feeling that her life was unexceptional. Holding her hands up in front of her face, Grace watched them tremble.

"So I'm going to be a grandmother again," Charlotte said. "That's nice."

"Great-grandmother."

"Whatever. For some people, it's hard to accept. They don't like it. When Lucy was born, I caught your father in the bathroom, tweezing white hairs from his chest."

Grace wasn't surprised to hear this. Her father had been very handsome, very vain. He looked at himself in store windows, rubbed oil into his face twice a day to keep his skin smooth. His face was always shiny; up close, he smelled sweetish, like limes, she remembered. He'd taught high-school French for nearly forty years and every year there were students in love with him. They baked him croissants, left him anonymous poems in French about the misery of unrequited love. He took these high-school girls very seriously, as if they were women whose love counted for something; when he died, Grace and her mother had found dozens of poems in an overnight bag hidden at the back of his closet. Sometimes the girls had been brave and come to the house, walking up and down the street in a group of three or four, hoping to see her father washing his car or mowing the lawn. If he happened to be out front, he would come down to the end of the driveway and tease them, always in French, using the names he'd given them in class—Lise, Martine, Hélène—cutting them off in midsentence when they tried to explain in English how they just happened to be in the neighborhood. *En français, mesdemoiselles.* Grace and her mother watched from the window enviously as her father performed for his students, turned on the charm for near-strangers who would forget all about him at the end of the school year. He had little of anything left over for his wife and daughter, had very little use for them, Grace always thought; he was a man in love with himself, unwilling to care deeply about anyone at all. That her mother had endured a long marriage to him still mystified her; that Alex had lately become someone whose weakness very nearly matched her father's was a greater irony than Grace ever could have imagined.

"Feeling better?" she asked Howard, who was slowly walking the length of the kitchen, his hands cupped at the small of his back. He kissed the tip of Grace's ear, then moved to the doorway and switched off the light. The plastic rose glowed between his teeth. "We can have our dinner by rose light," he said. "A rose-lit dinner."

"How about some coffee?" Grace said, turning the light back on. She returned to the counter and tossed the salad violently with a wooden spoon and fork. Pieces of lettuce flew over the top of the bowl and fell to the floor.

Howard blinked at her. "I'm trying to impress you," he said. "I've been trying to impress you for a long time now. Am I making a mistake?"

Charlotte laughed, then began to sing. Her voice was wobbly and high-pitched. "Mother mother mother pin a rose on me / Three young men are after me / One is blind, the others can't see / Mother mother mother pin a rose on me."

"Very funny," Howard said. "I refuse to take offense, Charlotte, because I know you like me and wouldn't dream of hurting my feelings."

Charlotte said, "I'm not picky. I liked all the boys my daughter brought home. Except for Alex, who proved what I've always known to be true, that you can wheel with people and deal with people, but never really know what they're thinking."

"I'd like to meet the man. I've heard very little about him, but I can't help thinking he's a screwed-up son of a bitch," Howard said. "What kind of man would actually choose to be alone, especially at his age? It's TV-dinner city, Johnny Carson for late-night company, and a sick feeling when you wake up in the morning."

"If you were sober," Grace said, "I'd tell you to shut up." She tossed the salad till her wrists ached; she rubbed first one and then the other with her thumbs.

"I'm telling you you don't love him. It's impossible to love someone who's willing to dismiss you like that, who hasn't the slightest interest in your well-being. It's an illusion, whatever it is you think you're feeling."

"An illusion," Charlotte said. "And how."

"The two of you should go into practice together," Grace said. "I could be the secretary-receptionist."

"You're disgusted with me. I see it in your eyes," Howard said sorrowfully.

"The eyes are the mirror of the soul," Charlotte said. "Your father's eyes, in fact, were colorless. I'd never seen eyes like that in my life. I should have known."

"What color are yours, Grace? May I look at them close up?" Howard approached her, squinting at her with one eye almost completely closed. He shook his head. "I could have sworn they were blue. Isn't that something? You think you know a person and then one day you realize their eyes aren't the color you thought they were."

Charlotte left her chair. "Let me see," she said. She stared at Grace for a moment, then said, "Did I forget your birthday again this year?"

"You're forgiven," Grace said.

"Not even a card?"

"When was this?" Howard said. "As close as we are, and you keep a secret like that from me."

"It was two weeks ago."

"Gee whiskers," Charlotte said. "Goddamnit."

She hadn't remembered Grace's birthday in years, not since Grace was a teenager. And every year Grace kept expecting a miracle. Stupid to care, but she did. Every year she felt let down, as if her mother had failed her in some important way. Alex used to threaten to send Charlotte an anonymous note warning her not to forget. She shouldn't have to be reminded, Grace would say. That's the whole point. Knowing how she felt, Alex had taken the trouble to send her a card this year, a gracious gesture, she told herself. When she'd taken the card from the mailbox, she'd held it in her hand for a moment, then run upstairs to the bathroom with it, locking the door behind her. She opened the envelope and stared at the silk-screened flowers, but would not open the card. She was expecting too much from him, and knew it. Whole paragraphs of passion and apology, confessions of stupidity and selfishness. She sat down at the edge of the bathtub and read what he'd written: *Happy Birthday.* He'd signed his name in a rush—the ink was smeared, the letters barely legible. She lingered over the card, wondering if he'd thought about saying more but caught himself in time. Holding the paper up to the light, she looked for something greater than what he'd given her, a message in invisible ink, perhaps.

"And I'm your mother," Charlotte said, sounding surprised. "It's not as if I'm some kind of casual acquaintance who didn't know any better."

"Thanks a lot," Howard said.

"Quiet," Grace said, thinking she'd heard something at the

side door. In the utility room off the kitchen, she turned on the outside light and looked out the door.

"How you doing?" Sean said. He was wearing a sweat shirt, running shorts, and rubber thongs. "I'm locked out. They're taking a shower and can't hear the doorbell."

"Aren't you cold, dressed like that?" Grace touched his thigh as they walked into the kitchen. His skin was cool but not icy. He looked perfectly healthy, as if his mother had been feeding him well whenever she happened to let him into the house.

"I'm pretty pissed off," Sean said. He didn't look unhappy, or even angry. He was a very patient child. Sometimes he rode his bicycle in endless circles out in the street in front of his house.

"Do I know you?" Howard said.

"I know *her,*" Sean said. "That's the lady who likes our garbage so much."

"I didn't recognize you without your bicycle," Charlotte said. "Where's your mother? Did she ever get dressed yesterday?"

"You know what? I may be seeing my father pretty soon," Sean said. He put his hand into the salad and took out a carrot curl. He looked at his hand; his face reddened. "I always do that at home," he said. "It's not the right thing to do, but I do it anyway."

Howard said, "Who's your father? Do I know him?"

"Have dinner with us if you're hungry. We'd be delighted to have you," Grace said.

"My father lives in Peru. On a pig farm."

"That was my first guess," Howard said. "A pig farm in Peru."

"He's in the Peace Corps," Sean said. "He's been there for two years and now he's coming home." He put the carrot into his mouth. "Can I use your phone?"

"Do you want me to dial the number for you?" Grace said.

"I'm not an idiot," Sean said. "I'm eleven years old." The rest of them fell silent as he made his call. "Twenty-five, six, seven, eight," he said, counting rings out loud. "Bingo. You locked me out again," he informed his mother. "I'm coming home in one minute and I'm going to ring the doorbell. I just wanted to warn you." He hung up the phone, shaking his head slowly. "What a birdbrain."

"Let me take you home. I wanted to talk to your mother, anyway," Grace said.

"No way, José. I'm not a baby." Sean picked out another carrot curl on his way to the door. "You should hear the way they sing in the shower," he confided to Grace, who had followed him out into the yard, into the moonlight. "I stand outside under the bathroom window sometimes and listen. They have such terrible voices, but they don't care. I saw a parrot last night on TV who sang this song, 'Bali Ha'i.' His voice was so good, a lot better than theirs." Sean's bare legs were white marble in the moonlight. "She's just a birdbrain," he said, as if to console her, and then he disappeared through an opening in the hedge that separated the two houses.


In the dining room, looking down the length of the table at the china and silverware and linen napkins, Grace had to acknowledge the satisfaction she always felt at things being in their rightful place. Over the years, Alex teased her for the way her hands automatically went out to straighten towels on racks, books in shelves, flowers in vases. A convention of Freudians would have a field day with you, he'd told her numerous times, but always lightly. Once, as a child, staying over at a cousin's house, Grace hadn't been able to fall asleep because the room was too messy. In the dark, while her cousin slept, Grace had cleaned up the room, picking clothing off the floor, shutting dresser drawers, arranging their slippers neatly next to their beds. The next morning she'd been too embarrassed to admit what she'd done, and pretended to her cousin she didn't know anything about it. Remembering this now, she laughed out loud.

"This is just great," Howard said. He was at the other end

of the table, miles from Grace, it seemed. "Sort of like Thanksgiving."

"I don't quite get the connection," Anthony said.

"Ditto," William said. Reaching into his brother's plate, he stole an olive. Anthony let it go, saying nothing. Like lovers, they'd been drinking from the same wineglass, finishing each other's sentences. When they were gone from the house, Grace would remember them as one person she would have liked to forget.

"I simply meant," Howard said, "that it had the feel of a nice family dinner."

Anthony said, "Ah yes, it seems like only yesterday. There we were: mother, father, two-point-three kids, dog, cat, fish tank, family-size car, Jell-O every night for dessert."

"We were never two-point-three kids," William said.

"Sometimes you seemed like three-point-two monkeys," Howard said. "Not that I'm complaining."

Grace was watching Lucy, who was sitting motionless in her seat, staring straight ahead at a framed watercolor on the wall. It was a drawing of a man in Elizabethan dress carrying a woman roughly over his shoulder—a poster advertising *The Taming of the Shrew.* "Lucy," Grace said. "What are you doing?"

"It's no wonder she has no appetite," Charlotte said. "Everything tastes like soap."

"Soap?"

"Detergent. Ivory Snow. Did you put Ivory Snow in the gravy instead of cornstarch?"

"Oh, that kind of soap. I couldn't imagine what kind of soap she was talking about," Howard said.

"Don't encourage her," Grace said. "Let's just change the subject."

"You can't fool me," Charlotte said, pushing her plate toward the center of the table. "My senses are sharp as a tack. But I can't for the life of me understand why anyone would invite people over for dinner and then serve them Ivory Snow."

William set his fork and knife neatly along his plate. "I can't eat any more. Not for a minute do I believe there's soap in this food. And yet . . ."

"The all-powerful power of suggestion," Anthony said, laying down his silverware. "Damn. And that roast beef was nice and rare, exactly the way I like it."

"You boys finish what's on your plates or there'll be no TV for a week," Howard said.

"Unless, of course, you were trying to poison me," Charlotte said slowly.

Howard said, "Poison? Isn't Ivory the soap they're always swearing is ninety-nine and forty-four one-hundredths percent pure?"

"Pure what?" Grace was laughing now, wild laughter that made her wheeze. She was a child misbehaving at the table; her mother glared at her.

"Lucrezia Borgia," Charlotte said.

Lucy tugged lightly at Grace's shirt collar. "I'm putting my Lamaze course to good use, if you really want to know. There's my focal point, right there." She motioned to the feather in the man's hat in *The Taming of the Shrew* poster.

"You're in labor?" Grace said, still laughing.

"Any time you want to be raced to the hospital, just let us know," William said.

Howard flicked two fingers against his water glass a few times. "Attention, please," he said. "I have a confession to make."

"If you're the father of this baby we don't want to hear about it."

"Actually, I've been taking sky-diving lessons. I didn't want to alarm anybody, so I've kept it a secret. Watch this." Howard threw off his shoes, got into a squat position on his chair, and, head tucked into his chest, rolled to the floor. The next moment he was sitting up saying, "Have I impressed you, Grace?"

"You're the furthest thing from her mind right now," Anthony said. "Let's pack you up and get you out of here."

"What about Lucy? Who's going to drive her to the hospital?" William said.

Anthony stood up and pulled his brother from his chair. "She doesn't even know you," he said. "You're a stranger. You don't fit in with her plans at all."

"The truth is," William said, shaking his head, "I wish I had gone to medical school. The law is a ass."

"Lucy," Grace said, "I know you don't want to be disturbed, but I need to talk to you."

"Don't ever interrupt me while I'm having a contraction," Lucy screamed at her. "You wrecked my concentration."

The twins had gotten Howard into his coat and were offering to come back later and move the rest of the furniture for Grace. Standing at the door in his tweed coat that had been buttoned up to his chin, Howard looked bewildered, and almost, Grace thought, as if he might weep.

"Please don't forget about me," he said in a tiny voice. "I just don't want to be forgotten."


The baby didn't have a name yet, though he was nearly a week old. Cliff had returned to California yesterday when he'd learned that his mother had died; Grace assumed they'd name the baby when he returned. He'd managed to miss the birth by just a couple of hours, and now, after a few days with his family, he was gone again. For Grace, his absence provided the perfect excuse to see Lucy and the baby, to help out at the house on the Maine coast that Lucy and Cliff had been renting since last fall. It was an impossibly small house with walls made of knotty pine and bare linoleum floors—a vacation house, really. But it was two hundred feet from the ocean and that, according to Lucy, was all that mattered.

Grace, behind the wheel of her station wagon with Alex beside her, tilted the rearview mirror again for another look at what was in the backseat: a stroller that folded almost to the size of an umbrella, a dark blue Silver Cross carriage (collapsed in a carton), a plastic swing that could be hung from any doorway, and an aluminum-and-canvas backpack to carry the baby around when he was older. Up front on the floor in a paper bag were packages of doll-size undershirts, some terry-cloth bibs (one which said "I Adore Grandma" on it), and a Fisher-Price Roly Poly Chime Ball.

"Are you driving or taking inventory?" Alex said, but it was clear from his voice that he was joking. Since the baby was born, he'd been in touch with Grace constantly—lots of phone calls back and forth, visits to the hospital together, even some leisurely lunches in a coffee shop near the hospital. At the restaurant, each time he'd picked up the check and helped Grace into her coat, she'd felt as if they were out on a date, as if, like a suitor, he'd been trying to please her in small ways. His suggestion, late last night over the phone, that he drive up to Maine with her, had caught her by surprise. Immediately she'd wondered about the sleeping arrangements, pictured the two of them in bed with an imaginary line drawn down the length of it, a line neither of them would feel free to cross. They had slept in a bed together, been beneath each other's clothes a lifetime ago, it seemed. When (or if ) it happened again, she would accept it as the miracle that was her due.

When they'd seen the baby for the first time, Alex's eyes had filled with tears, but hers had not. She was too busy studying his face, looking for proof that he needed to connect again, that he was willing to acknowledge who he really was. She wanted to see if he was ready to trade the perfect silence for something less comfortable, for a place within a family; the most imperfect of worlds, she had to admit. Like it or not, he was middle-aged, graying, ordinary—categories he slipped easily into and had not been able to find a way out of. He'd tried to blame her for who he was, pretending that he could no longer afford to waste his time with her. Well, she had news for him: with or without her, he was as he'd always been—a little less sympathetic than she'd hoped for, a little too fond of solitude, a little too pessimistic, but still someone she could love. Watching his grandson asleep on his side in the glassed-in nursery, Alex worried out loud about the baby's broad, crooked nose and the small red bruises that marked his cheeks. Grace had to work hard to convince him that the baby would look one hundred percent better the next day, two hundred percent better the day after that.

"You want me to drive?" he asked her now. He leaned forward in his seat and fooled around with the radio, trying to get a Boston station.

"I hate to break it to you," Grace said, "but you're a terrible driver." For as long as she'd known him, he'd been exasperating in the driver's seat, slow and wandering, so preoccupied she always assumed he did his deepest thinking behind the wheel.

"Am I?" Alex said. "How come I've never had an accident?"

"You've been lucky, I guess."

"Why bring it up at this late date?"

Funny, she thought, that he wasn't interested in knowing exactly what he'd been doing wrong all these years. "I've gotten pretty brazen in my old age," Grace said.

"You," Alex said, and then he was silent.

"What about me?"

"How did you get to be a grandmother?"

"It happens," Grace said.

"I don't like thinking of you that way."

"You don't like thinking of yourself that way." Her father, frantic, tweezing the white from his chest.

Alex shut the radio off. He flipped up the collar of his coat, stared into his lap. "What will happen to me?" he said.

"You tell me." Her stomach felt hollow; she listened for the sounds of hunger, but there weren't any. Through the windshield, which was streaked with a smashed insect or two and a thin grayish film, the day, at noon, looked more overcast than it really was. It was April now, but still wintry; her hands resting on the steering wheel were winter hands, dry and white, powdery between her fingers. Lucy's house would be chilly, cold enough to have a fire going in the fireplace at nightfall. She could see herself standing at the living room window that faced the ocean, watching the surfers in their wet suits, giant arctic creatures in shining black rubber crouched on their boards for what seemed to be only a moment before they vanished into the dark water. She and Alex would take the obligatory walk along the beach every afternoon, keeping their eyes open for the unexpected: months ago, soon after Lucy had moved to the shore, she and Lucy had found an underwater camera that had washed up on the rocks—a small bright yellow camera that had probably slipped through someone's hands during the summer; Grace had never seen anything like it.

Alex was talking to her. "We could try again," he was saying into the collar of his coat. "We could make promises and try to keep them."

She lifted a hand from the steering wheel and turned back his collar. "If you like," she said. She was amazed at how casual she was able to sound, as casual as if she'd been offered an umbrella in a fine, warm rain, the sort of rain you almost didn't want to be sheltered from.

"I want to take you somewhere," Alex said.

"Paris?" Grace said. "A week in Paris could be very therapeutic."

"Let's get off at this exit right up here." He pointed to a sign that promised food, fuel, and lodging.

"Here?" She was already turning off the highway and could see, in the distance, the orange roof of a Howard Johnson's, and beyond it, a McDonald's and a Dunkin' Donuts. Depressing, predictable territory. "A two-and-a-half-hour trip doesn't require a rest stop," Grace said. "Not unless it's an emergency."

"Slow down," Alex said as they approached the Howard Johnson's. There was a two-story motel attached to it; the parking lot just outside the row of rooms was nearly empty.

"It's very urgent that we talk," he said. "We'll get a room and talk things through."

She pulled the car into a space in front of the restaurant, but left the motor running. "Not on the first date, I don't," she said.

Alex had the door open and one foot touching the pavement. "In that case, we could live together," he said. "And if it works out, we could even get married, have a child, grandchildren . . ."

"I've been there," Grace said. "What else can you offer me?"

"Don't be greedy," Alex said.

He turned to smile at her, then dropped his other foot to the ground. He stood up and slammed the door shut. Outside, his back against the car, his arms folded at his waist, he waited for her. She imagined the gradual darkening of the sky, the appearance of a clear bright moon and stars. In the moonlight, he waited for her, crazy as a man in love.